# TEACHER'S PET PUBLICATIONS

## PUZZLE PACK
for
The Odyssey

based on the work by
Homer

Written by
William T. Collins

© 2005 Teacher's Pet Publications
All Rights Reserved

The materials in this packet are copyrighted
by Teacher's Pet Publications, Inc.

These pages may be duplicated by the purchaser
for use in the purchaser's own classroom.

Copying any of these materials and distributing them
for any other purpose is a violation of the copyright laws.

© 2005 Teacher's Pet Publications, Inc.
www.tpet.com

## INTRODUCTION
If you already own the LitPlan for this title, this Puzzle Pack will refresh your Unit Resource Materials and Vocabulary Resource Materials sections plus give you additional materials you can substitute into the tests. If you do not already have a complete LitPlan, these pages will give you some supplemental materials to use with your own plan. There are two main groups of materials: one set for unit words (such as characters' names, symbols, places, etc.) and one set for vocabulary words associated with the book.

## WORD LIST
There is a word list for both the unit words and the vocabulary words. These lists show you which words are being used in the materials and the clues or definitions being used for those words. You may want to give students a word list with clues/definitions to help them, or you may want students to only have a word list (without clues/definitions) if you want them to work a little harder. Both are available for duplication. The word lists can also be your "calling key" for the bingo games.

## FILL IN THE BLANK AND MATCHING
There are 4 each of the fill in the blank and matching worksheets for both the unit and vocabulary words. These pages can be used either as extra worksheets for students or as objective parts of a unit test. They can be done individually if students need extra help or as a whole class activity to review the material covered.

## MAGIC SQUARES
The magic squares not only reinforce the material covered but also work on reasoning and math skills. Many teachers have told us that their students really enjoy doing these!

## WORD SEARCH PUZZLES
The word search words go in all directions, as indicated on your answer keys. Two of the word search puzzles have the clues listed rather than the words. This makes the puzzle a little more difficult, but it reinforces the material better. Two word search puzzles have words only for students who find the clue puzzles too difficult.

## CROSSWORD PUZZLES
Both unit and vocabulary word sections have 4 crossword puzzles.

## BINGO CARDS
There are 32 individual bingo cards for the unit words and 32 individual bingo cards for the vocabulary words. You can use your word list as a "call list," calling the words at random and marking them off of your list as you go, or you could use the flash cards by cutting them apart and drawing the words at random from a hat (or box or whatever). To make a better review, you might ask for the definition and spelling of each word as you call it out–or you could call out the definitions and have students tell you the words they need to look for on the puzzle.

## JUGGLE LETTERS
The vocabulary juggle letter game is intended to help students learn the spellings of the words. One sheet has the definitions listed on it as an extra help for students who need it or to reinforce the definitions if you choose to do so.

## FLASH CARDS
We've included a set of vocabulary flash cards you can duplicate, cut, and fold for your students. Some teachers make a few sets for general use by the class; others make a set for each student. Some teachers duplicate them for each student and have the students cut & fold their own. You can cut out just the words and put them in a hat, have each student pick out one word and write the definition and a sentence for that word. Students then swap words and papers, with the next student adding a sentence of his own under the last one. You can have students swap as many times as you like. Each time the student will read the sentences written prior to his own and then add a sentence. You can cut out the words and definitions separately and play "I Have; Who Has?" Each student in the room draws a word and definition. The first student says, "I have (the name of the word). Who has the definition?" The student with the definition reads it then says, "I have (the name of the vocabulary word she has). Who has the definition?" The round continues until all words and definitions have been given.

**Odyssey Word List**

| No. | Word | Clue/Definition |
|---|---|---|
| 1. | AEOLUS | A mortal to whom the gods have given control of the winds |
| 2. | AGAMEMNON | King of Mycene; murdered by his wife & her lover |
| 3. | AKHAIANS | One of Homer's names for the Greeks |
| 4. | ARGUS | Odysseus's dog |
| 5. | CROSSBOW | Weapon of Odysseus |
| 6. | DISCUS | Plate-like object that is thrown in contests |
| 7. | EAGLE | Bird often used as omen |
| 8. | ELPENOR | One of Odysseus' crew; fell from Kirke's roof |
| 9. | EUMAEUS | Odysseus' faithful swineherd |
| 10. | EURYKLEIA | Nurse for both Odysseus & Telemakhos |
| 11. | EURYMACHOS | One of the suitors; threw a stool at Odysseus |
| 12. | GIFTS | They were important to the Greeks; presents |
| 13. | HADES | Ruler of the underworld; brother to Zeus and Poseidon |
| 14. | HELEN | Wife of Menelaus; the Prince of Troy abducted her |
| 15. | HELIOS | God of the sun; owner of cattle |
| 16. | INO | Goddess who gave Odysseus her veil |
| 17. | ITHAKA | Native land and home of Odysseus |
| 18. | KALYPSO | Goddess who kept Odysseus on her island for years |
| 19. | KHARYBDIS | Whirlpool that sucked down ship and crewmen |
| 20. | KIRKE | Goddess who tried to turn Odysseus & crew into pigs |
| 21. | KLYTIAMNESTRA | Wife and murderer of Agamemnon |
| 22. | KYKLOPES | The one-eyed giants |
| 23. | LAERTES | Father of Odysseus |
| 24. | LAESTRYGONIANS | Race of cannibals |
| 25. | MENELAUS | Helen's husband; King of Sparta |
| 26. | MENTOR | A visitor in Ithaka; really Athena disguised |
| 27. | NAUSIKAA | Daughter of the King of Phaikia |
| 28. | NESTOR | King of Pylos; reminisces about the good old days |
| 29. | ODYSSEUS | Hero of the Trojan War who goes on a journey |
| 30. | OMEN | Sign of good or bad luck to come |
| 31. | ORESTES | Agamemnon's son |
| 32. | PENELOPE | Faithful wife of Odysseus |
| 33. | POLYPHEMOS | Kyklops who captured Odysseus & his men |
| 34. | POSEIDON | God of the sea; seeks revenge on Odysseus for blinding his son |
| 35. | SCAR | Means by which which Odysseus is recognized by nurse |
| 36. | SEIRINES | Nymphs whose singing entices men to land on their island |
| 37. | SKHERIA | Home of the Phaikians |
| 38. | SKYLLA | Six-headed monster |
| 39. | SUITORS | The men who wanted to marry Penelope |
| 40. | TEIRESIAS | Blind prophet whom Odysseus visited in the underworld |
| 41. | TELEMAKHOS | Son of Odysseus |
| 42. | UNDERWORLD | Guarded by Hades; the place where the dead go |
| 43. | ZEUS | King of the gods; lives on Mt. Olympus |

Odyssey Fill In The Blanks 1

_____  1. Faithful wife of Odysseus

_____  2. One of the suitors; threw a stool at Odysseus

_____  3. One of Homer's names for the Greeks

_____  4. Nurse for both Odysseus & Telemakhos

_____  5. Goddess who kept Odysseus on her island for years

_____  6. Helen's husband; King of Sparta

_____  7. Wife and murderer of Agamemnon

_____  8. Wife of Menelaus; the Prince of Troy abducted her

_____  9. God of the sun; owner of cattle

_____ 10. Daughter of the King of Phaikia

_____ 11. King of Pylos; reminisces about the good old days

_____ 12. Nymphs whose singing entices men to land on their island

_____ 13. Blind prophet whom Odysseus visited in the underworld

_____ 14. A mortal to whom the gods have given control of the winds

_____ 15. Hero of the Trojan War who goes on a journey

_____ 16. The one-eyed giants

_____ 17. Agamemnon's son

_____ 18. Odysseus's dog

_____ 19. Goddess who gave Odysseus her veil

_____ 20. Father of Odysseus

Odyssey Fill In The Blanks 1 Answer Key

| | |
|---|---|
| PENELOPE | 1. Faithful wife of Odysseus |
| EURYMACHOS | 2. One of the suitors; threw a stool at Odysseus |
| AKHAIANS | 3. One of Homer's names for the Greeks |
| EURYKLEIA | 4. Nurse for both Odysseus & Telemakhos |
| KALYPSO | 5. Goddess who kept Odysseus on her island for years |
| MENELAUS | 6. Helen's husband; King of Sparta |
| KLYTIAMNESTRA | 7. Wife and murderer of Agamemnon |
| HELEN | 8. Wife of Menelaus; the Prince of Troy abducted her |
| HELIOS | 9. God of the sun; owner of cattle |
| NAUSIKAA | 10. Daughter of the King of Phaikia |
| NESTOR | 11. King of Pylos; reminisces about the good old days |
| SEIRINES | 12. Nymphs whose singing entices men to land on their island |
| TEIRESIAS | 13. Blind prophet whom Odysseus visited in the underworld |
| AEOLUS | 14. A mortal to whom the gods have given control of the winds |
| ODYSSEUS | 15. Hero of the Trojan War who goes on a journey |
| KYKLOPES | 16. The one-eyed giants |
| ORESTES | 17. Agamemnon's son |
| ARGUS | 18. Odysseus's dog |
| INO | 19. Goddess who gave Odysseus her veil |
| LAERTES | 20. Father of Odysseus |

Odyssey Fill In The Blanks 2

_____

_____

_____

_____

_____

_____

_____

_____

_____

_____

_____

_____

_____

_____

_____

_____

_____

_____

_____

_____

1. Hero of the Trojan War who goes on a journey
2. One of Homer's names for the Greeks
3. Odysseus's dog
4. Father of Odysseus
5. One of Odysseus' crew; fell from Kirke's roof
6. Goddess who gave Odysseus her veil
7. They were important to the Greeks; presents
8. Home of the Phaikians
9. Six-headed monster
10. Bird often used as omen
11. Whirlpool that sucked down ship and crewmen
12. Ruler of the underworld; brother to Zeus and Poseidon
13. Faithful wife of Odysseus
14. King of the gods; lives on Mt. Olympus
15. Wife and murderer of Agamemnon
16. Kyklops who captured Odysseus & his men
17. The men who wanted to marry Penelope
18. Guarded by Hades; the place where the dead go
19. Blind prophet whom Odysseus visited in the underworld
20. God of the sun; owner of cattle

Odyssey Fill In The Blanks 2 Answer Key

| | |
|---|---|
| ODYSSEUS | 1. Hero of the Trojan War who goes on a journey |
| AKHAIANS | 2. One of Homer's names for the Greeks |
| ARGUS | 3. Odysseus's dog |
| LAERTES | 4. Father of Odysseus |
| ELPENOR | 5. One of Odysseus' crew; fell from Kirke's roof |
| INO | 6. Goddess who gave Odysseus her veil |
| GIFTS | 7. They were important to the Greeks; presents |
| SKHERIA | 8. Home of the Phaikians |
| SKYLLA | 9. Six-headed monster |
| EAGLE | 10. Bird often used as omen |
| KHARYBDIS | 11. Whirlpool that sucked down ship and crewmen |
| HADES | 12. Ruler of the underworld; brother to Zeus and Poseidon |
| PENELOPE | 13. Faithful wife of Odysseus |
| ZEUS | 14. King of the gods; lives on Mt. Olympus |
| KLYTIAMNESTRA | 15. Wife and murderer of Agamemnon |
| POLYPHEMOS | 16. Kyklops who captured Odysseus & his men |
| SUITORS | 17. The men who wanted to marry Penelope |
| UNDERWORLD | 18. Guarded by Hades; the place where the dead go |
| TEIRESIAS | 19. Blind prophet whom Odysseus visited in the underworld |
| HELIOS | 20. God of the sun; owner of cattle |

Odyssey Fill In The Blanks 3

_____

1. A visitor in Ithaka; really Athena disguised
2. Goddess who kept Odysseus on her island for years
3. Odysseus' faithful swineherd
4. Blind prophet whom Odysseus visited in the underworld
5. Goddess who tried to turn Odysseus & crew into pigs
6. A mortal to whom the gods have given control of the winds
7. Means by which which Odysseus is recognized by nurse
8. Sign of good or bad luck to come
9. Six-headed monster
10. Guarded by Hades; the place where the dead go
11. Father of Odysseus
12. Native land and home of Odysseus
13. King of Pylos; reminisces about the good old days
14. Helen's husband; King of Sparta
15. Weapon of Odysseus
16. Daughter of the King of Phaikia
17. God of the sea; seeks revenge on Odysseus for blinding his son
18. Wife of Menelaus; the Prince of Troy abducted her
19. Nurse for both Odysseus & Telemakhos
20. One of Odysseus' crew; fell from Kirke's roof

Odyssey Fill In The Blanks 3 Answer Key

| | |
|---|---|
| MENTOR | 1. A visitor in Ithaka; really Athena disguised |
| KALYPSO | 2. Goddess who kept Odysseus on her island for years |
| EUMAEUS | 3. Odysseus' faithful swineherd |
| TEIRESIAS | 4. Blind prophet whom Odysseus visited in the underworld |
| KIRKE | 5. Goddess who tried to turn Odysseus & crew into pigs |
| AEOLUS | 6. A mortal to whom the gods have given control of the winds |
| SCAR | 7. Means by which which Odysseus is recognized by nurse |
| OMEN | 8. Sign of good or bad luck to come |
| SKYLLA | 9. Six-headed monster |
| UNDERWORLD | 10. Guarded by Hades; the place where the dead go |
| LAERTES | 11. Father of Odysseus |
| ITHAKA | 12. Native land and home of Odysseus |
| NESTOR | 13. King of Pylos; reminisces about the good old days |
| MENELAUS | 14. Helen's husband; King of Sparta |
| CROSSBOW | 15. Weapon of Odysseus |
| NAUSIKAA | 16. Daughter of the King of Phaikia |
| POSEIDON | 17. God of the sea; seeks revenge on Odysseus for blinding his son |
| HELEN | 18. Wife of Menelaus; the Prince of Troy abducted her |
| EURYKLEIA | 19. Nurse for both Odysseus & Telemakhos |
| ELPENOR | 20. One of Odysseus' crew; fell from Kirke's roof |

Odyssey Fill In The Blanks 4

_____    1. Goddess who tried to turn Odysseus & crew into pigs

_____    2. The men who wanted to marry Penelope

_____    3. Six-headed monster

_____    4. Nurse for both Odysseus & Telemakhos

_____    5. Agamemnon's son

_____    6. Plate-like object that is thrown in contests

_____    7. Goddess who gave Odysseus her veil

_____    8. Whirlpool that sucked down ship and crewmen

_____    9. Goddess who kept Odysseus on her island for years

_____    10. King of Mycene; murdered by his wife & her lover

_____    11. King of Pylos; reminisces about the good old days

_____    12. Sign of good or bad luck to come

_____    13. Wife and murderer of Agamemnon

_____    14. Son of Odysseus

_____    15. Wife of Menelaus; the Prince of Troy abducted her

_____    16. Helen's husband; King of Sparta

_____    17. Father of Odysseus

_____    18. Daughter of the King of Phaikia

_____    19. Odysseus's dog

_____    20. Bird often used as omen

Odyssey Fill In The Blanks 4 Answer Key

| Answer | Clue |
|---|---|
| KIRKE | 1. Goddess who tried to turn Odysseus & crew into pigs |
| SUITORS | 2. The men who wanted to marry Penelope |
| SKYLLA | 3. Six-headed monster |
| EURYKLEIA | 4. Nurse for both Odysseus & Telemakhos |
| ORESTES | 5. Agamemnon's son |
| DISCUS | 6. Plate-like object that is thrown in contests |
| INO | 7. Goddess who gave Odysseus her veil |
| KHARYBDIS | 8. Whirlpool that sucked down ship and crewmen |
| KALYPSO | 9. Goddess who kept Odysseus on her island for years |
| AGAMEMNON | 10. King of Mycene; murdered by his wife & her lover |
| NESTOR | 11. King of Pylos; reminisces about the good old days |
| OMEN | 12. Sign of good or bad luck to come |
| KLYTIAMNESTRA | 13. Wife and murderer of Agamemnon |
| TELEMAKHOS | 14. Son of Odysseus |
| HELEN | 15. Wife of Menelaus; the Prince of Troy abducted her |
| MENELAUS | 16. Helen's husband; King of Sparta |
| LAERTES | 17. Father of Odysseus |
| NAUSIKAA | 18. Daughter of the King of Phaikia |
| ARGUS | 19. Odysseus's dog |
| EAGLE | 20. Bird often used as omen |

Odyssey Matching 1

___ 1. KALYPSO
___ 2. HELIOS
___ 3. KLYTIAMNESTRA
___ 4. ARGUS
___ 5. ORESTES
___ 6. EURYMACHOS
___ 7. KYKLOPES
___ 8. ODYSSEUS
___ 9. EAGLE
___ 10. GIFTS
___ 11. NESTOR
___ 12. KIRKE
___ 13. CROSSBOW
___ 14. AEOLUS
___ 15. LAESTRYGONIANS
___ 16. ELPENOR
___ 17. ITHAKA
___ 18. SEIRINES
___ 19. MENELAUS
___ 20. INO
___ 21. DISCUS
___ 22. SKHERIA
___ 23. LAERTES
___ 24. EURYKLEIA
___ 25. MENTOR

A. Agamemnon's son
B. Helen's husband; King of Sparta
C. Father of Odysseus
D. A mortal to whom the gods have given control of the winds
E. Home of the Phaikians
F. Race of cannibals
G. Plate-like object that is thrown in contests
H. Bird often used as omen
I. They were important to the Greeks; presents
J. The one-eyed giants
K. King of Pylos; reminisces about the good old days
L. Wife and murderer of Agamemnon
M. Native land and home of Odysseus
N. Nurse for both Odysseus & Telemakhos
O. A visitor in Ithaka; really Athena disguised
P. Nymphs whose singing entices men to land on their island
Q. One of Odysseus' crew; fell from Kirke's roof
R. Weapon of Odysseus
S. Hero of the Trojan War who goes on a journey
T. Goddess who tried to turn Odysseus & crew into pigs
U. God of the sun; owner of cattle
V. Goddess who gave Odysseus her veil
W. Odysseus's dog
X. Goddess who kept Odysseus on her island for years
Y. One of the suitors; threw a stool at Odysseus

Odyssey Matching 1 Answer Key

| | |
|---|---|
| X - 1. KALYPSO | A. Agamemnon's son |
| U - 2. HELIOS | B. Helen's husband; King of Sparta |
| L - 3. KLYTIAMNESTRA | C. Father of Odysseus |
| W - 4. ARGUS | D. A mortal to whom the gods have given control of the winds |
| A - 5. ORESTES | E. Home of the Phaikians |
| Y - 6. EURYMACHOS | F. Race of cannibals |
| J - 7. KYKLOPES | G. Plate-like object that is thrown in contests |
| S - 8. ODYSSEUS | H. Bird often used as omen |
| H - 9. EAGLE | I. They were important to the Greeks; presents |
| I - 10. GIFTS | J. The one-eyed giants |
| K - 11. NESTOR | K. King of Pylos; reminisces about the good old days |
| T - 12. KIRKE | L. Wife and murderer of Agamemnon |
| R - 13. CROSSBOW | M. Native land and home of Odysseus |
| D - 14. AEOLUS | N. Nurse for both Odysseus & Telemakhos |
| F - 15. LAESTRYGONIANS | O. A visitor in Ithaka; really Athena disguised |
| Q - 16. ELPENOR | P. Nymphs whose singing entices men to land on their island |
| M - 17. ITHAKA | Q. One of Odysseus' crew; fell from Kirke's roof |
| P - 18. SEIRINES | R. Weapon of Odysseus |
| B - 19. MENELAUS | S. Hero of the Trojan War who goes on a journey |
| V - 20. INO | T. Goddess who tried to turn Odysseus & crew into pigs |
| G - 21. DISCUS | U. God of the sun; owner of cattle |
| E - 22. SKHERIA | V. Goddess who gave Odysseus her veil |
| C - 23. LAERTES | W. Odysseus's dog |
| N - 24. EURYKLEIA | X. Goddess who kept Odysseus on her island for years |
| O - 25. MENTOR | Y. One of the suitors; threw a stool at Odysseus |

Odyssey Matching 2

___ 1. HELIOS
___ 2. EUMAEUS
___ 3. ITHAKA
___ 4. KALYPSO
___ 5. INO
___ 6. AKHAIANS
___ 7. MENTOR
___ 8. HELEN
___ 9. KHARYBDIS
___ 10. DISCUS
___ 11. POSEIDON
___ 12. EURYMACHOS
___ 13. LAERTES
___ 14. OMEN
___ 15. SKHERIA
___ 16. AGAMEMNON
___ 17. SKYLLA
___ 18. TEIRESIAS
___ 19. MENELAUS
___ 20. ELPENOR
___ 21. GIFTS
___ 22. SUITORS
___ 23. NESTOR
___ 24. KYKLOPES
___ 25. EAGLE

A. King of Mycene; murdered by his wife & her lover
B. They were important to the Greeks; presents
C. Goddess who kept Odysseus on her island for years
D. Bird often used as omen
E. The one-eyed giants
F. God of the sun; owner of cattle
G. Plate-like object that is thrown in contests
H. God of the sea; seeks revenge on Odysseus for blinding his son
I. Blind prophet whom Odysseus visited in the underworld
J. Six-headed monster
K. Father of Odysseus
L. King of Pylos; reminisces about the good old days
M. Odysseus' faithful swineherd
N. Wife of Menelaus; the Prince of Troy abducted her
O. The men who wanted to marry Penelope
P. Goddess who gave Odysseus her veil
Q. One of Homer's names for the Greeks
R. Home of the Phaikians
S. Native land and home of Odysseus
T. One of the suitors; threw a stool at Odysseus
U. Whirlpool that sucked down ship and crewmen
V. Sign of good or bad luck to come
W. A visitor in Ithaka; really Athena disguised
X. One of Odysseus' crew; fell from Kirke's roof
Y. Helen's husband; King of Sparta

## Odyssey Matching 2 Answer Key

| | | |
|---|---|---|
| F - 1. HELIOS | A. | King of Mycene; murdered by his wife & her lover |
| M - 2. EUMAEUS | B. | They were important to the Greeks; presents |
| S - 3. ITHAKA | C. | Goddess who kept Odysseus on her island for years |
| C - 4. KALYPSO | D. | Bird often used as omen |
| P - 5. INO | E. | The one-eyed giants |
| Q - 6. AKHAIANS | F. | God of the sun; owner of cattle |
| W - 7. MENTOR | G. | Plate-like object that is thrown in contests |
| N - 8. HELEN | H. | God of the sea; seeks revenge on Odysseus for blinding his son |
| U - 9. KHARYBDIS | I. | Blind prophet whom Odysseus visited in the underworld |
| G - 10. DISCUS | J. | Six-headed monster |
| H - 11. POSEIDON | K. | Father of Odysseus |
| T - 12. EURYMACHOS | L. | King of Pylos; reminisces about the good old days |
| K - 13. LAERTES | M. | Odysseus' faithful swineherd |
| V - 14. OMEN | N. | Wife of Menelaus; the Prince of Troy abducted her |
| R - 15. SKHERIA | O. | The men who wanted to marry Penelope |
| A - 16. AGAMEMNON | P. | Goddess who gave Odysseus her veil |
| J - 17. SKYLLA | Q. | One of Homer's names for the Greeks |
| I - 18. TEIRESIAS | R. | Home of the Phaikians |
| Y - 19. MENELAUS | S. | Native land and home of Odysseus |
| X - 20. ELPENOR | T. | One of the suitors; threw a stool at Odysseus |
| B - 21. GIFTS | U. | Whirlpool that sucked down ship and crewmen |
| O - 22. SUITORS | V. | Sign of good or bad luck to come |
| L - 23. NESTOR | W. | A visitor in Ithaka; really Athena disguised |
| E - 24. KYKLOPES | X. | One of Odysseus' crew; fell from Kirke's roof |
| D - 25. EAGLE | Y. | Helen's husband; King of Sparta |

Odyssey Matching 3

___ 1. TELEMAKHOS  A. Guarded by Hades; the place where the dead go
___ 2. SEIRINES  B. Wife of Menelaus; the Prince of Troy abducted her
___ 3. KLYTIAMNESTRA  C. One of Odysseus' crew; fell from Kirke's roof
___ 4. NAUSIKAA  D. Goddess who kept Odysseus on her island for years
___ 5. CROSSBOW  E. Nymphs whose singing entices men to land on their island
___ 6. EAGLE  F. Means by which which Odysseus is recognized by nurse
___ 7. EURYMACHOS  G. Odysseus's dog
___ 8. AGAMEMNON  H. Bird often used as omen
___ 9. OMEN  I. Son of Odysseus
___10. KALYPSO  J. King of Mycene; murdered by his wife & her lover
___11. DISCUS  K. Daughter of the King of Phaikia
___12. UNDERWORLD  L. Nurse for both Odysseus & Telemakhos
___13. ARGUS  M. The one-eyed giants
___14. AKHAIANS  N. Ruler of the underworld; brother to Zeus and Poseidon
___15. LAERTES  O. Agamemnon's son
___16. MENELAUS  P. Sign of good or bad luck to come
___17. SUITORS  Q. Weapon of Odysseus
___18. KYKLOPES  R. A visitor in Ithaka; really Athena disguised
___19. ORESTES  S. Father of Odysseus
___20. MENTOR  T. Plate-like object that is thrown in contests
___21. EURYKLEIA  U. One of the suitors; threw a stool at Odysseus
___22. HELEN  V. The men who wanted to marry Penelope
___23. ELPENOR  W. Helen's husband; King of Sparta
___24. HADES  X. One of Homer's names for the Greeks
___25. SCAR  Y. Wife and murderer of Agamemnon

Odyssey Matching 3 Answer Key

| | | |
|---|---|---|
| I - 1. TELEMAKHOS | A. | Guarded by Hades; the place where the dead go |
| E - 2. SEIRINES | B. | Wife of Menelaus; the Prince of Troy abducted her |
| Y - 3. KLYTIAMNESTRA | C. | One of Odysseus' crew; fell from Kirke's roof |
| K - 4. NAUSIKAA | D. | Goddess who kept Odysseus on her island for years |
| Q - 5. CROSSBOW | E. | Nymphs whose singing entices men to land on their island |
| H - 6. EAGLE | F. | Means by which which Odysseus is recognized by nurse |
| U - 7. EURYMACHOS | G. | Odysseus's dog |
| J - 8. AGAMEMNON | H. | Bird often used as omen |
| P - 9. OMEN | I. | Son of Odysseus |
| D - 10. KALYPSO | J. | King of Mycene; murdered by his wife & her lover |
| T - 11. DISCUS | K. | Daughter of the King of Phaikia |
| A - 12. UNDERWORLD | L. | Nurse for both Odysseus & Telemakhos |
| G - 13. ARGUS | M. | The one-eyed giants |
| X - 14. AKHAIANS | N. | Ruler of the underworld; brother to Zeus and Poseidon |
| S - 15. LAERTES | O. | Agamemnon's son |
| W - 16. MENELAUS | P. | Sign of good or bad luck to come |
| V - 17. SUITORS | Q. | Weapon of Odysseus |
| M - 18. KYKLOPES | R. | A visitor in Ithaka; really Athena disguised |
| O - 19. ORESTES | S. | Father of Odysseus |
| R - 20. MENTOR | T. | Plate-like object that is thrown in contests |
| L - 21. EURYKLEIA | U. | One of the suitors; threw a stool at Odysseus |
| B - 22. HELEN | V. | The men who wanted to marry Penelope |
| C - 23. ELPENOR | W. | Helen's husband; King of Sparta |
| N - 24. HADES | X. | One of Homer's names for the Greeks |
| F - 25. SCAR | Y. | Wife and murderer of Agamemnon |

Copyrighted

Odyssey Matching 4

___ 1. ELPENOR
___ 2. OMEN
___ 3. ORESTES
___ 4. GIFTS
___ 5. ARGUS
___ 6. NESTOR
___ 7. EUMAEUS
___ 8. POSEIDON
___ 9. TEIRESIAS
___ 10. EAGLE
___ 11. INO
___ 12. KIRKE
___ 13. LAESTRYGONIANS
___ 14. KHARYBDIS
___ 15. SKHERIA
___ 16. KYKLOPES
___ 17. ITHAKA
___ 18. TELEMAKHOS
___ 19. SKYLLA
___ 20. POLYPHEMOS
___ 21. AKHAIANS
___ 22. MENELAUS
___ 23. DISCUS
___ 24. ZEUS
___ 25. KALYPSO

A. They were important to the Greeks; presents
B. Kyklops who captured Odysseus & his men
C. Race of cannibals
D. Sign of good or bad luck to come
E. One of Homer's names for the Greeks
F. The one-eyed giants
G. Agamemnon's son
H. Goddess who gave Odysseus her veil
I. King of the gods; lives on Mt. Olympus
J. Bird often used as omen
K. Odysseus' faithful swineherd
L. Goddess who tried to turn Odysseus & crew into pigs
M. Whirlpool that sucked down ship and crewmen
N. Son of Odysseus
O. One of Odysseus' crew; fell from Kirke's roof
P. Plate-like object that is thrown in contests
Q. Helen's husband; King of Sparta
R. Home of the Phaikians
S. King of Pylos; reminisces about the good old days
T. Blind prophet whom Odysseus visited in the underworld
U. Goddess who kept Odysseus on her island for years
V. Odysseus's dog
W. Native land and home of Odysseus
X. Six-headed monster
Y. God of the sea; seeks revenge on Odysseus for blinding his son

Odyssey Matching 4 Answer Key

| | |
|---|---|
| O - 1. ELPENOR | A. They were important to the Greeks; presents |
| D - 2. OMEN | B. Kyklops who captured Odysseus & his men |
| G - 3. ORESTES | C. Race of cannibals |
| A - 4. GIFTS | D. Sign of good or bad luck to come |
| V - 5. ARGUS | E. One of Homer's names for the Greeks |
| S - 6. NESTOR | F. The one-eyed giants |
| K - 7. EUMAEUS | G. Agamemnon's son |
| Y - 8. POSEIDON | H. Goddess who gave Odysseus her veil |
| T - 9. TEIRESIAS | I. King of the gods; lives on Mt. Olympus |
| J - 10. EAGLE | J. Bird often used as omen |
| H - 11. INO | K. Odysseus' faithful swineherd |
| L - 12. KIRKE | L. Goddess who tried to turn Odysseus & crew into pigs |
| C - 13. LAESTRYGONIANS | M. Whirlpool that sucked down ship and crewmen |
| M - 14. KHARYBDIS | N. Son of Odysseus |
| R - 15. SKHERIA | O. One of Odysseus' crew; fell from Kirke's roof |
| F - 16. KYKLOPES | P. Plate-like object that is thrown in contests |
| W - 17. ITHAKA | Q. Helen's husband; King of Sparta |
| N - 18. TELEMAKHOS | R. Home of the Phaikians |
| X - 19. SKYLLA | S. King of Pylos; reminisces about the good old days |
| B - 20. POLYPHEMOS | T. Blind prophet whom Odysseus visited in the underworld |
| E - 21. AKHAIANS | U. Goddess who kept Odysseus on her island for years |
| Q - 22. MENELAUS | V. Odysseus's dog |
| P - 23. DISCUS | W. Native land and home of Odysseus |
| I - 24. ZEUS | X. Six-headed monster |
| U - 25. KALYPSO | Y. God of the sea; seeks revenge on Odysseus for blinding his son |

Odyssey Magic Squares 1

Match the definition with the vocabulary word. Put your answers in the magic squares below. When your answers are correct, all columns and rows will add to the same number.

A. SEIRINES
B. TELEMAKHOS
C. KHARYBDIS
D. CROSSBOW
E. TEIRESIAS
F. NAUSIKAA
G. NESTOR
H. ODYSSEUS
I. AGAMEMNON
J. LAERTES
K. ZEUS
L. KIRKE
M. ELPENOR
N. EURYKLEIA
O. ARGUS
P. PENELOPE

1. Daughter of the King of Phaikia
2. King of Mycene; murdered by his wife & her lover
3. Odysseus's dog
4. Weapon of Odysseus
5. One of Odysseus' crew; fell from Kirke's roof
6. Son of Odysseus
7. Hero of the Trojan War who goes on a journey
8. King of the gods; lives on Mt. Olympus
9. Whirlpool that sucked down ship and crewmen
10. Faithful wife of Odysseus
11. Father of Odysseus
12. Blind prophet whom Odysseus visited in the underworld
13. Goddess who tried to turn Odysseus & crew into pigs
14. King of Pylos; reminisces about the good old days
15. Nymphs whose singing entices men to land on their island
16. Nurse for both Odysseus & Telemakhos

| A= | B= | C= | D= |
|---|---|---|---|
| E= | F= | G= | H= |
| I= | J= | K= | L= |
| M= | N= | O= | P= |

Odyssey Magic Squares 1 Answer Key

Match the definition with the vocabulary word. Put your answers in the magic squares below. When your answers are correct, all columns and rows will add to the same number.

A. SEIRINES
B. TELEMAKHOS
C. KHARYBDIS
D. CROSSBOW
E. TEIRESIAS
F. NAUSIKAA
G. NESTOR
H. ODYSSEUS
I. AGAMEMNON
J. LAERTES
K. ZEUS
L. KIRKE
M. ELPENOR
N. EURYKLEIA
O. ARGUS
P. PENELOPE

1. Daughter of the King of Phaikia
2. King of Mycene; murdered by his wife & her lover
3. Odysseus's dog
4. Weapon of Odysseus
5. One of Odysseus' crew; fell from Kirke's roof
6. Son of Odysseus
7. Hero of the Trojan War who goes on a journey
8. King of the gods; lives on Mt. Olympus
9. Whirlpool that sucked down ship and crewmen
10. Faithful wife of Odysseus
11. Father of Odysseus
12. Blind prophet whom Odysseus visited in the underworld
13. Goddess who tried to turn Odysseus & crew into pigs
14. King of Pylos; reminisces about the good old days
15. Nymphs whose singing entices men to land on their island
16. Nurse for both Odysseus & Telemakhos

| A=15 | B=6 | C=9 | D=4 |
| --- | --- | --- | --- |
| E=12 | F=1 | G=14 | H=7 |
| I=2 | J=11 | K=8 | L=13 |
| M=5 | N=16 | O=3 | P=10 |

Odyssey Magic Squares 2

Match the definition with the vocabulary word. Put your answers in the magic squares below. When your answers are correct, all columns and rows will add to the same number.

A. HADES
B. EURYKLEIA
C. ZEUS
D. KALYPSO
E. POLYPHEMOS
F. EAGLE
G. TELEMAKHOS
H. NAUSIKAA
I. INO
J. KYKLOPES
K. AKHAIANS
L. KLYTIAMNESTRA
M. SUITORS
N. SCAR
O. AEOLUS
P. EURYMACHOS

1. Nurse for both Odysseus & Telemakhos
2. Son of Odysseus
3. One of Homer's names for the Greeks
4. Means by which which Odysseus is recognized by nurse
5. The men who wanted to marry Penelope
6. Wife and murderer of Agamemnon
7. Daughter of the King of Phaikia
8. Ruler of the underworld; brother to Zeus and Poseidon
9. One of the suitors; threw a stool at Odysseus
10. Goddess who gave Odysseus her veil
11. Kyklops who captured Odysseus & his men
12. Goddess who kept Odysseus on her island for years
13. King of the gods; lives on Mt. Olympus
14. Bird often used as omen
15. The one-eyed giants
16. A mortal to whom the gods have given control of the winds

| A= | B= | C= | D= |
|---|---|---|---|
| E= | F= | G= | H= |
| I= | J= | K= | L= |
| M= | N= | O= | P= |

# Odyssey Magic Squares 2 Answer Key

Match the definition with the vocabulary word. Put your answers in the magic squares below. When your answers are correct, all columns and rows will add to the same number.

A. HADES
B. EURYKLEIA
C. ZEUS
D. KALYPSO
E. POLYPHEMOS
F. EAGLE
G. TELEMAKHOS
H. NAUSIKAA
I. INO
J. KYKLOPES
K. AKHAIANS
L. KLYTIAMNESTRA
M. SUITORS
N. SCAR
O. AEOLUS
P. EURYMACHOS

1. Nurse for both Odysseus & Telemakhos
2. Son of Odysseus
3. One of Homer's names for the Greeks
4. Means by which which Odysseus is recognized by nurse
5. The men who wanted to marry Penelope
6. Wife and murderer of Agamemnon
7. Daughter of the King of Phaikia
8. Ruler of the underworld; brother to Zeus and Poseidon
9. One of the suitors; threw a stool at Odysseus
10. Goddess who gave Odysseus her veil
11. Kyklops who captured Odysseus & his men
12. Goddess who kept Odysseus on her island for years
13. King of the gods; lives on Mt. Olympus
14. Bird often used as omen
15. The one-eyed giants
16. A mortal to whom the gods have given control of the winds

| A=8 | B=1 | C=13 | D=12 |
|---|---|---|---|
| E=11 | F=14 | G=2 | H=7 |
| I=10 | J=15 | K=3 | L=6 |
| M=5 | N=4 | O=16 | P=9 |

Odyssey Magic Squares 3

Match the definition with the vocabulary word. Put your answers in the magic squares below. When your answers are correct, all columns and rows will add to the same number.

A. INO
B. EUMAEUS
C. EURYMACHOS
D. DISCUS
E. CROSSBOW
F. SEIRINES
G. SCAR
H. KHARYBDIS
I. UNDERWORLD
J. SKHERIA
K. AKHAIANS
L. ORESTES
M. PENELOPE
N. ZEUS
O. KALYPSO
P. HADES

1. Whirlpool that sucked down ship and crewmen
2. Faithful wife of Odysseus
3. Odysseus' faithful swineherd
4. One of Homer's names for the Greeks
5. Home of the Phaikians
6. One of the suitors; threw a stool at Odysseus
7. Ruler of the underworld; brother to Zeus and Poseidon
8. Weapon of Odysseus
9. Goddess who kept Odysseus on her island for years
10. Nymphs whose singing entices men to land on their island
11. Guarded by Hades; the place where the dead go
12. Plate-like object that is thrown in contests
13. Goddess who gave Odysseus her veil
14. Agamemnon's son
15. Means by which which Odysseus is recognized by nurse
16. King of the gods; lives on Mt. Olympus

| A= | B= | C= | D= |
|---|---|---|---|
| E= | F= | G= | H= |
| I= | J= | K= | L= |
| M= | N= | O= | P= |

25
Copyrighted

Odyssey Magic Squares 3 Answer Key

Match the definition with the vocabulary word. Put your answers in the magic squares below. When your answers are correct, all columns and rows will add to the same number.

A. INO
B. EUMAEUS
C. EURYMACHOS
D. DISCUS
E. CROSSBOW
F. SEIRINES
G. SCAR
H. KHARYBDIS
I. UNDERWORLD
J. SKHERIA
K. AKHAIANS
L. ORESTES
M. PENELOPE
N. ZEUS
O. KALYPSO
P. HADES

1. Whirlpool that sucked down ship and crewmen
2. Faithful wife of Odysseus
3. Odysseus' faithful swineherd
4. One of Homer's names for the Greeks
5. Home of the Phaikians
6. One of the suitors; threw a stool at Odysseus
7. Ruler of the underworld; brother to Zeus and Poseidon
8. Weapon of Odysseus
9. Goddess who kept Odysseus on her island for years
10. Nymphs whose singing entices men to land on their island
11. Guarded by Hades; the place where the dead go
12. Plate-like object that is thrown in contests
13. Goddess who gave Odysseus her veil
14. Agamemnon's son
15. Means by which which Odysseus is recognized by nurse
16. King of the gods; lives on Mt. Olympus

| A=13 | B=3 | C=6 | D=12 |
| --- | --- | --- | --- |
| E=8 | F=10 | G=15 | H=1 |
| I=11 | J=5 | K=4 | L=14 |
| M=2 | N=16 | O=9 | P=7 |

Odyssey Magic Squares 4

Match the definition with the vocabulary word. Put your answers in the magic squares below. When your answers are correct, all columns and rows will add to the same number.

A. SKHERIA
B. INO
C. TEIRESIAS
D. AEOLUS
E. MENELAUS
F. ZEUS
G. EAGLE
H. NAUSIKAA
I. ITHAKA
J. SUITORS
K. LAERTES
L. EUMAEUS
M. UNDERWORLD
N. EURYMACHOS
O. ODYSSEUS
P. POSEIDON

1. One of the suitors; threw a stool at Odysseus
2. Bird often used as omen
3. Odysseus' faithful swineherd
4. Home of the Phaikians
5. Father of Odysseus
6. Goddess who gave Odysseus her veil
7. Guarded by Hades; the place where the dead go
8. Daughter of the King of Phaikia
9. Helen's husband; King of Sparta
10. God of the sea; seeks revenge on Odysseus for blinding his son
11. Blind prophet whom Odysseus visited in the underworld
12. The men who wanted to marry Penelope
13. A mortal to whom the gods have given control of the winds
14. Native land and home of Odysseus
15. King of the gods; lives on Mt. Olympus
16. Hero of the Trojan War who goes on a journey

| A= | B= | C= | D= |
|---|---|---|---|
| E= | F= | G= | H= |
| I= | J= | K= | L= |
| M= | N= | O= | P= |

Odyssey Magic Squares 4 Answer Key

Match the definition with the vocabulary word. Put your answers in the magic squares below. When your answers are correct, all columns and rows will add to the same number.

A. SKHERIA
B. INO
C. TEIRESIAS
D. AEOLUS
E. MENELAUS
F. ZEUS
G. EAGLE
H. NAUSIKAA
I. ITHAKA
J. SUITORS
K. LAERTES
L. EUMAEUS
M. UNDERWORLD
N. EURYMACHOS
O. ODYSSEUS
P. POSEIDON

1. One of the suitors; threw a stool at Odysseus
2. Bird often used as omen
3. Odysseus' faithful swineherd
4. Home of the Phaikians
5. Father of Odysseus
6. Goddess who gave Odysseus her veil
7. Guarded by Hades; the place where the dead go
8. Daughter of the King of Phaikia
9. Helen's husband; King of Sparta
10. God of the sea; seeks revenge on Odysseus for blinding his son
11. Blind prophet whom Odysseus visited in the underworld
12. The men who wanted to marry Penelope
13. A mortal to whom the gods have given control of the winds
14. Native land and home of Odysseus
15. King of the gods; lives on Mt. Olympus
16. Hero of the Trojan War who goes on a journey

| A=4 | B=6 | C=11 | D=13 |
|---|---|---|---|
| E=9 | F=15 | G=2 | H=8 |
| I=14 | J=12 | K=5 | L=3 |
| M=7 | N=1 | O=16 | P=10 |

Odyssey Word Search 1

Words are placed backwards, forward, diagonally, up and down. Clues listed below can help you find the words. Circle the hidden vocabulary words in the maze.

```
K H A R Y B D I S L E U M A E U S C
W E Z W T A T K Y A P S U I T O R S
B L T N M E C T R E O L A E R T E S
K E O P Q O N J S S L B G K T P E C
H N Y R C J A B T E S W A D U D K
T Z W C E U I W R N K B L R E C M
G A R G U S O N L Y E S K Y L A Y
P N S S E B T M V G P M K P J P S Y
W D R R S G G E E O H L H S M E X S
J Q I S A S M S S N E A B O I N O V
D E O S U K U S O I E P D M P O Q P
T R H E C E H D A A L P E G R K B
C N Z E S U I A V N G G A N S A Y E
L S E S L E S T I S L I M U W I K V
S F Y S S I H C H A E F E R S R L M
C D W O T V O P A A N T N W I E O D
O B P W K O P S D R K S T K P H P M
L F S E N I R I E S D A O H C K E Q
Y K L Y T I A M N E S T R A F S S S
```

A mortal to whom the gods have given control of the winds (6)
A visitor in Ithaka; really Athena disguised (6)
Agamemnon's son (7)
Bird often used as omen (5)
Blind prophet whom Odysseus visited in the underworld (9)
Faithful wife of Odysseus (8)
Father of Odysseus (7)
God of the sea; seeks revenge on Odysseus for blinding his son (8)
God of the sun; owner of cattle (6)
Goddess who gave Odysseus her veil (3)
Goddess who kept Odysseus on her island for years (7)
Goddess who tried to turn Odysseus & crew into pigs (5)
Helen's husband; King of Sparta (8)
Hero of the Trojan War who goes on a journey (8)
Home of the Phaikians (7)
King of Pylos; reminisces about the good old days (6)
King of the gods; lives on Mt. Olympus (4)
Means by which which Odysseus is recognized by nurse (4)
Native land and home of Odysseus (6)
Nurse for both Odysseus & Telemakhos (9)
Nymphs whose singing entices men to land on their island (8)
Odysseus' faithful swineherd (7)
Odysseus's dog (5)
One of Homer's names for the Greeks (8)
One of Odysseus' crew; fell from Kirke's roof (7)
Plate-like object that is thrown in contests (6)
Race of cannibals (14)
Ruler of the underworld; brother to Zeus and Poseidon (5)
Sign of good or bad luck to come (4)
Six-headed monster (6)
The men who wanted to marry Penelope (7)
The one-eyed giants (8)
They were important to the Greeks; presents (5)
Weapon of Odysseus (8)
Whirlpool that sucked down ship and crewmen (9)
Wife and murderer of Agamemnon (13)
Wife of Menelaus; the Prince of Troy abducted her (5)

Odyssey Word Search 1 Answer Key

Words are placed backwards, forward, diagonally, up and down. Clues listed below can help you find the words. Circle the hidden vocabulary words in the maze.

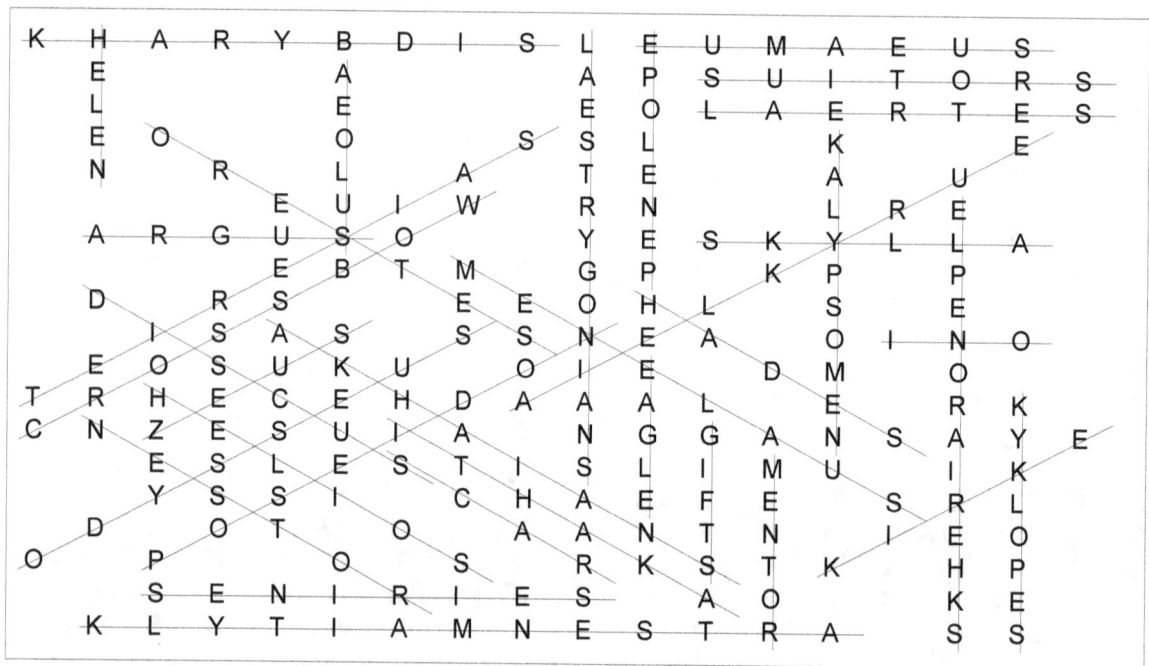

A mortal to whom the gods have given control of the winds (6)
A visitor in Ithaka; really Athena disguised (6)
Agamemnon's son (7)
Bird often used as omen (5)
Blind prophet whom Odysseus visited in the underworld (9)
Faithful wife of Odysseus (8)
Father of Odysseus (7)
God of the sea; seeks revenge on Odysseus for blinding his son (8)
God of the sun; owner of cattle (6)
Goddess who gave Odysseus her veil (3)
Goddess who kept Odysseus on her island for years (7)
Goddess who tried to turn Odysseus & crew into pigs (5)
Helen's husband; King of Sparta (8)
Hero of the Trojan War who goes on a journey (8)
Home of the Phaikians (7)
King of Pylos; reminisces about the good old days (6)
King of the gods; lives on Mt. Olympus (4)
Means by which which Odysseus is recognized by nurse (4)
Native land and home of Odysseus (6)
Nurse for both Odysseus & Telemakhos (9)
Nymphs whose singing entices men to land on their island (8)
Odysseus' faithful swineherd (7)
Odysseus's dog (5)
One of Homer's names for the Greeks (8)
One of Odysseus' crew; fell from Kirke's roof (7)
Plate-like object that is thrown in contests (6)
Race of cannibals (14)
Ruler of the underworld; brother to Zeus and Poseidon (5)
Sign of good or bad luck to come (4)
Six-headed monster (6)
The men who wanted to marry Penelope (7)
The one-eyed giants (8)
They were important to the Greeks; presents (5)
Weapon of Odysseus (8)
Whirlpool that sucked down ship and crewmen (9)
Wife and murderer of Agamemnon (13)
Wife of Menelaus; the Prince of Troy abducted her (5)

Odyssey Word Search 2

Words are placed backwards, forward, diagonally, up and down. Clues listed below can help you find the words. Circle the hidden vocabulary words in the maze.

```
P O S E I D O N E O D Y S S E U S T
G G V T S A A C U S N D P C S S S B
K C J J M U G X R V K F P A Z I S C
N Y H X S S L A Y O G H R R F D P Y
O T K I Q Y K K M V S P E Z P B G M
Y R K L C H A J A E I S V R T Y W H
S A E S O D W K C T M H B R I R Q Y
A J D S S P D L H M E N T O R A E G
T Z S N T V E A O A E D O V W H A C
A F Y E L E K S S L I Y T N J K G D
A R W K L A S O E L M A Q D J F L X
L X G Y X P N H C D S E N I R I E S
L R F U D I E K J U U G K S E M H S
Y C Z Z S H M N L R I I A C U J E B
K I R K E N O O T T F L U M D L D
S Z B M K U E T Y R O T Y S A D I G
J S C B F A S C W H R S P H E R O R
C S E T R E A L B S S S S B U C S C
K S P E N E L O P E T M O Y S R S P
```

A mortal to whom the gods have given control of the winds (6)
A visitor in Ithaka; really Athena disguised (6)
Agamemnon's son (7)
Bird often used as omen (5)
Daughter of the King of Phaikia (8)
Faithful wife of Odysseus (8)
Father of Odysseus (7)
God of the sea; seeks revenge on Odysseus for blinding his son (8)
God of the sun; owner of cattle (6)
Goddess who gave Odysseus her veil (3)
Goddess who kept Odysseus on her island for years (7)
Goddess who tried to turn Odysseus & crew into pigs (5)
Hero of the Trojan War who goes on a journey (8)
Home of the Phaikians (7)
King of Mycene; murdered by his wife & her lover (9)
King of Pylos; reminisces about the good old days (6)
King of the gods; lives on Mt. Olympus (4)
Means by which which Odysseus is recognized by nurse (4)
Native land and home of Odysseus (6)
Nymphs whose singing entices men to land on their island (8)
Odysseus' faithful swineherd (7)
Odysseus's dog (5)
One of Homer's names for the Greeks (8)
One of Odysseus' crew; fell from Kirke's roof (7)
One of the suitors; threw a stool at Odysseus (10)
Plate-like object that is thrown in contests (6)
Ruler of the underworld; brother to Zeus and Poseidon (5)
Sign of good or bad luck to come (4)
Six-headed monster (6)
The men who wanted to marry Penelope (7)
The one-eyed giants (8)
They were important to the Greeks; presents (5)
Weapon of Odysseus (8)
Whirlpool that sucked down ship and crewmen (9)
Wife of Menelaus; the Prince of Troy abducted her (5)

Odyssey Word Search 2 Answer Key

Words are placed backwards, forward, diagonally, up and down. Clues listed below can help you find the words. Circle the hidden vocabulary words in the maze.

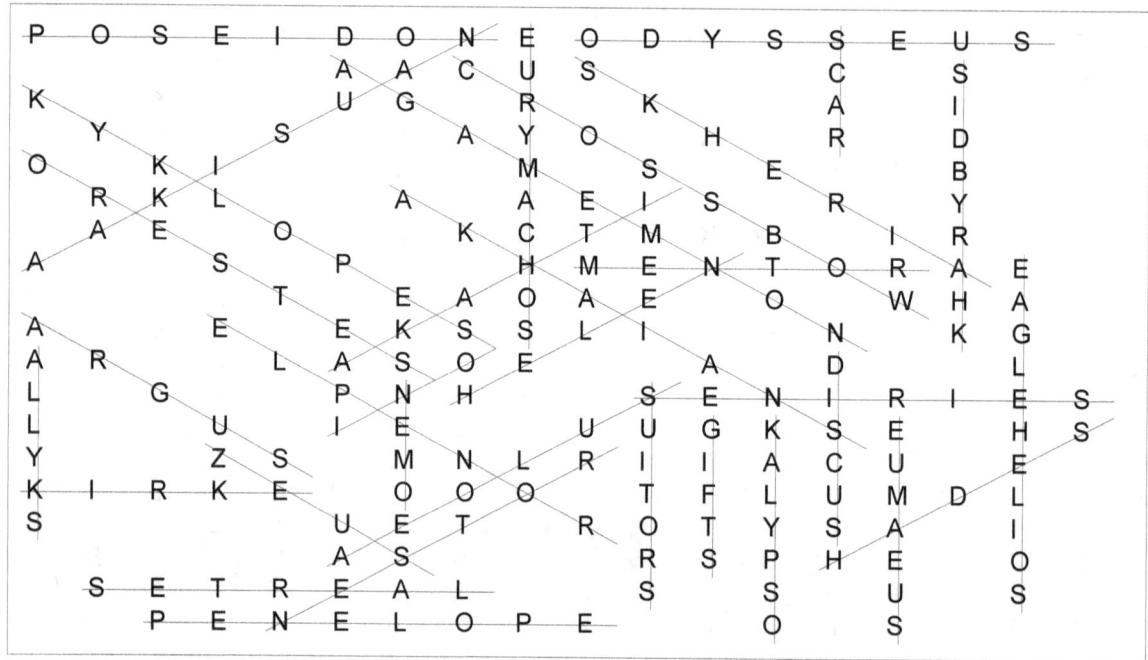

A mortal to whom the gods have given control of the winds (6)
A visitor in Ithaka; really Athena disguised (6)
Agamemnon's son (7)
Bird often used as omen (5)
Daughter of the King of Phaikia (8)
Faithful wife of Odysseus (8)
Father of Odysseus (7)
God of the sea; seeks revenge on Odysseus for blinding his son (8)
God of the sun; owner of cattle (6)
Goddess who gave Odysseus her veil (3)
Goddess who kept Odysseus on her island for years (7)
Goddess who tried to turn Odysseus & crew into pigs (5)
Hero of the Trojan War who goes on a journey (8)
Home of the Phaikians (7)
King of Mycene; murdered by his wife & her lover (9)
King of Pylos; reminisces about the good old days (6)
King of the gods; lives on Mt. Olympus (4)
Means by which which Odysseus is recognized by nurse (4)
Native land and home of Odysseus (6)
Nymphs whose singing entices men to land on their island (8)
Odysseus' faithful swineherd (7)
Odysseus's dog (5)
One of Homer's names for the Greeks (8)
One of Odysseus' crew; fell from Kirke's roof (7)
One of the suitors; threw a stool at Odysseus (10)
Plate-like object that is thrown in contests (6)
Ruler of the underworld; brother to Zeus and Poseidon (5)
Sign of good or bad luck to come (4)
Six-headed monster (6)
The men who wanted to marry Penelope (7)
The one-eyed giants (8)
They were important to the Greeks; presents (5)
Weapon of Odysseus (8)
Whirlpool that sucked down ship and crewmen (9)
Wife of Menelaus; the Prince of Troy abducted her (5)

Odyssey Word Search 3

Words are placed backwards, forward, diagonally, up and down. Words listed below are included in the maze. Circle the hidden vocabulary words in the maze.

```
M O D Y S S E U S Y M E N E L A U S
B E U R Y K L E I A Q O D I S C U S
Q W G E Y H Q F V V N C M F N J G S K
S P M W U E X H G M S N A I A H K A
E C S E I R I N E S N A U S I K A A M
L R A W Q I Y M E L O C G N N H G M
P O L R M A A M L U E M O B O A I K
E S N F S G M U A L M N E C G R F S
N S E D A H E N P C A A J N Y Y T F W
O B Y L I K S D E P H E E G R B S W
R O L J S I T E N O K O R U T D O P
O W R Q E R O R E S K L S T S I H T
T R J C R K W L E K U E Z E S K M
N C E V I E D O O I A S P E A S A V
E Z C S E L Y R P D L G O U L K M C
M N F H T J G L E O Y G L S S Y E L
W S O I L E H D L N P Z K E Z L V V
S U I T O R S B C G S C Y S H L E T
I T H A K A R G U S O R K J T A T V
```

| AEOLUS | HELIOS | OMEN |
| AGAMEMNON | INO | ORESTES |
| AKHAIANS | ITHAKA | PENELOPE |
| ARGUS | KALYPSO | POSEIDON |
| CROSSBOW | KHARYBDIS | SCAR |
| DISCUS | KIRKE | SEIRINES |
| EAGLE | KYKLOPES | SKHERIA |
| ELPENOR | LAERTES | SKYLLA |
| EUMAEUS | LAESTRYGONIANS | SUITORS |
| EURYKLEIA | MENELAUS | TEIRESIAS |
| EURYMACHOS | MENTOR | TELEMAKHOS |
| GIFTS | NAUSIKAA | UNDERWORLD |
| HADES | NESTOR | ZEUS |
| HELEN | ODYSSEUS | |

Odyssey Word Search 3 Answer Key

Words are placed backwards, forward, diagonally, up and down. Words listed below are included in the maze. Circle the hidden vocabulary words in the maze.

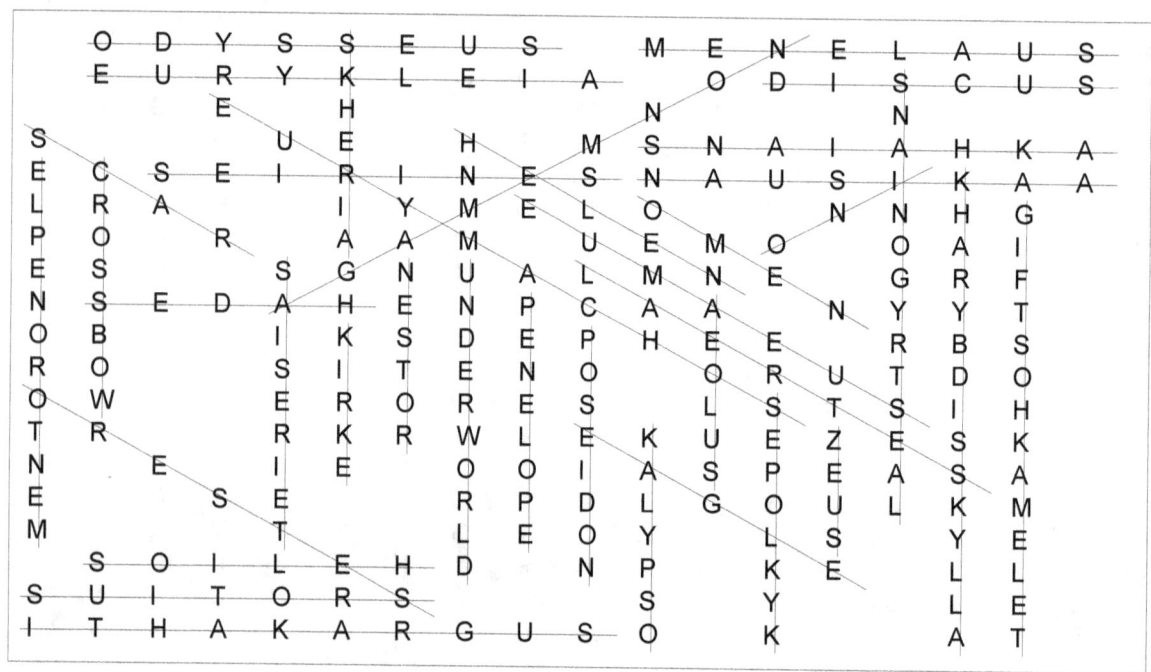

| AEOLUS | HELIOS | OMEN |
| --- | --- | --- |
| AGAMEMNON | INO | ORESTES |
| AKHAIANS | ITHAKA | PENELOPE |
| ARGUS | KALYPSO | POSEIDON |
| CROSSBOW | KHARYBDIS | SCAR |
| DISCUS | KIRKE | SEIRINES |
| EAGLE | KYKLOPES | SKHERIA |
| ELPENOR | LAERTES | SKYLLA |
| EUMAEUS | LAESTRYGONIANS | SUITORS |
| EURYKLEIA | MENELAUS | TEIRESIAS |
| EURYMACHOS | MENTOR | TELEMAKHOS |
| GIFTS | NAUSIKAA | UNDERWORLD |
| HADES | NESTOR | ZEUS |
| HELEN | ODYSSEUS | |

## Odyssey Word Search 4

Words are placed backwards, forward, diagonally, up and down. Words listed below are included in the maze. Circle the hidden vocabulary words in the maze.

```
H P O S E I D O N K A L Y P S O A G
U E H S L N O M E M A G R I P F
T N L M N N N A U S A V M K M Y
E C D M E O L C P I N E L O E
L D T E M I S C H E L G D P G
E D W E R F P R A V H M I K T
M U G M P W D I E T K S R F C K
A M M K D R J O N O S Y L T Y L Z
K R X H H R O E A E R C K K Y D O
H X D A L A E T L S U E S T J V S
O E T R E C G I E X E Y I R Y E L
S Q F B B U O E X D R J A P W D L G
E S B D I N S T H X H L M O M E L P D
P U S I E A G L E N E R H Z T N P Z
O I C T Z B K L A N T X L J N Z
L T A H E V I R E B S L H R O M
K O R S A U O K S Q T O T S E N R K
Y R T J K H Q T X R J R E K R G W T
K S O H C A M Y R U E Q S B Q Y H D
```

| | | |
|---|---|---|
| AEOLUS | INO | ORESTES |
| AGAMEMNON | ITHAKA | PENELOPE |
| ARGUS | KALYPSO | POSEIDON |
| DISCUS | KHARYBDIS | SCAR |
| EAGLE | KIRKE | SEIRINES |
| ELPENOR | KLYTIAMNESTRA | SKHERIA |
| EUMAEUS | KYKLOPES | SKYLLA |
| EURYKLEIA | LAERTES | SUITORS |
| EURYMACHOS | MENELAUS | TEIRESIAS |
| GIFTS | MENTOR | TELEMAKHOS |
| HADES | NESTOR | UNDERWORLD |
| HELEN | ODYSSEUS | ZEUS |
| HELIOS | OMEN | |

Odyssey Word Search 4 Answer Key

Words are placed backwards, forward, diagonally, up and down. Words listed below are included in the maze. Circle the hidden vocabulary words in the maze.

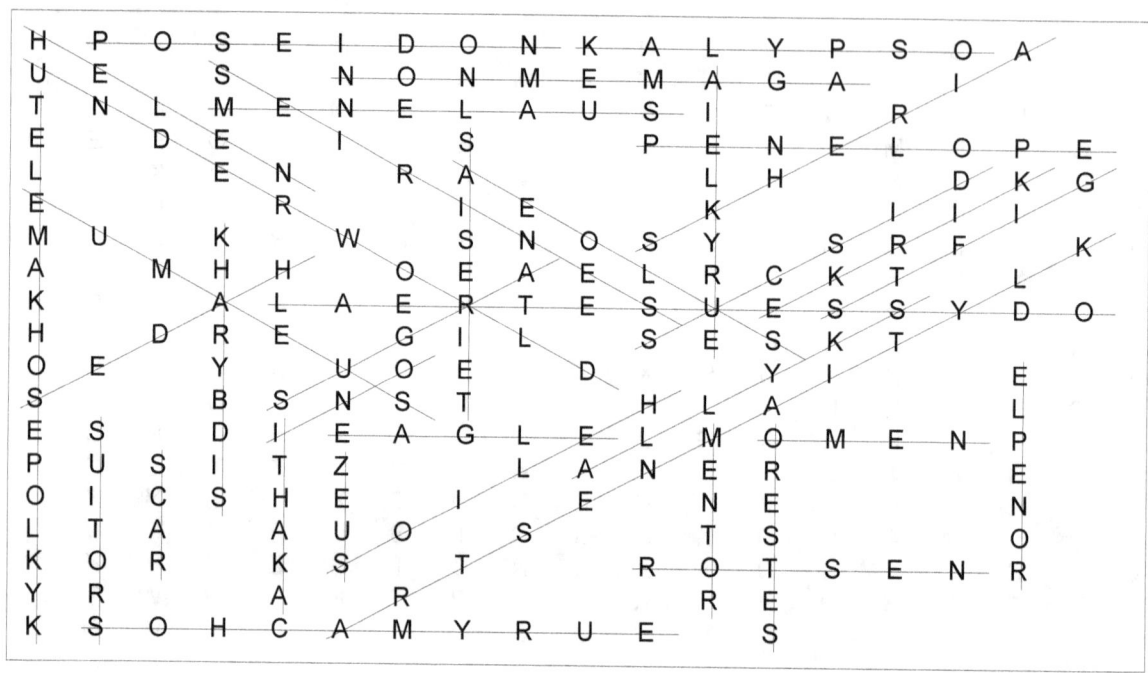

| AEOLUS | INO | ORESTES |
| AGAMEMNON | ITHAKA | PENELOPE |
| ARGUS | KALYPSO | POSEIDON |
| DISCUS | KHARYBDIS | SCAR |
| EAGLE | KIRKE | SEIRINES |
| ELPENOR | KLYTIAMNESTRA | SKHERIA |
| EUMAEUS | KYKLOPES | SKYLLA |
| EURYKLEIA | LAERTES | SUITORS |
| EURYMACHOS | MENELAUS | TEIRESIAS |
| GIFTS | MENTOR | TELEMAKHOS |
| HADES | NESTOR | UNDERWORLD |
| HELEN | ODYSSEUS | ZEUS |
| HELIOS | OMEN | |

# Odyssey Crossword 1

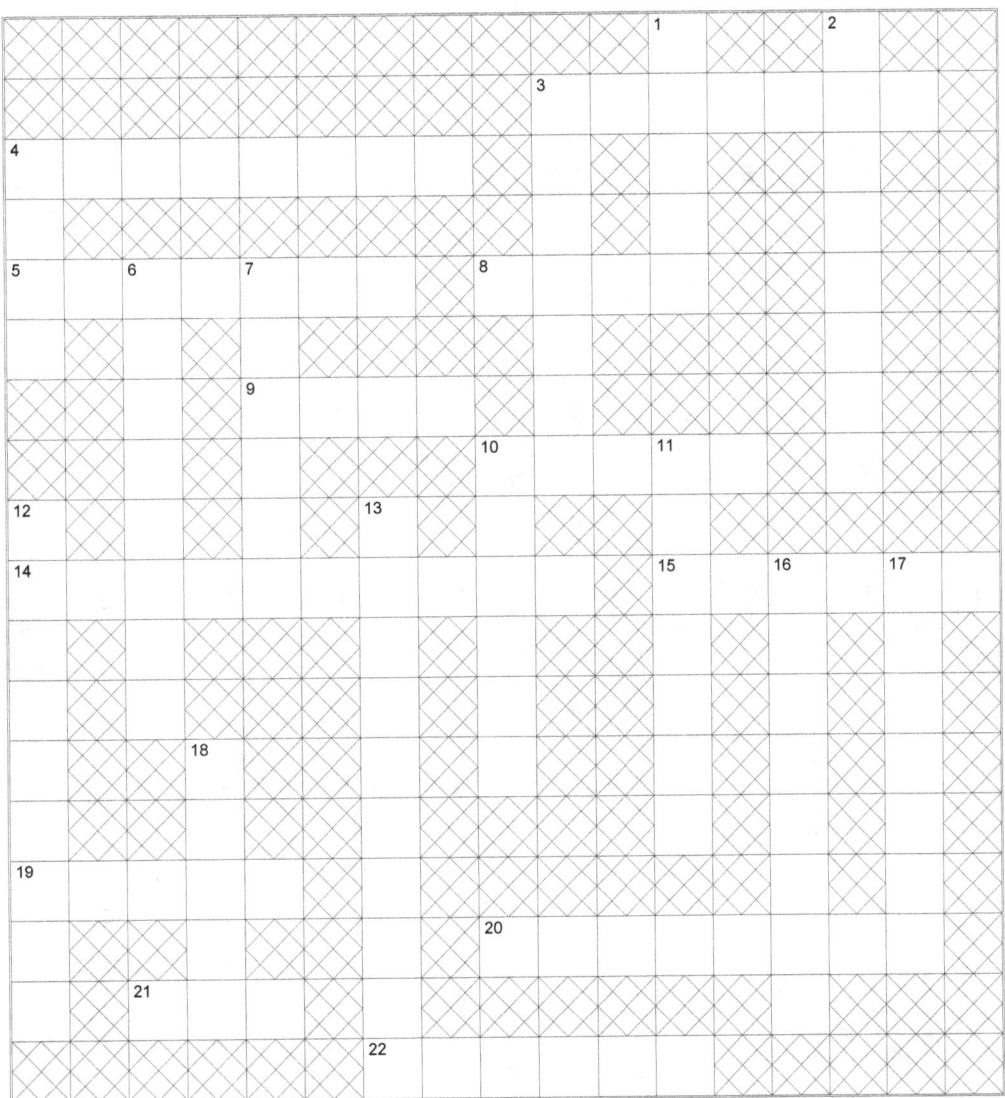

**Across**

3. The men who wanted to marry Penelope
4. Hero of the Trojan War who goes on a journey
5. One of Odysseus' crew; fell from Kirke's roof
8. King of the gods; lives on Mt. Olympus
9. Means by which which Odysseus is recognized by nurse
10. Ruler of the underworld; brother to Zeus and Poseidon
14. Guarded by Hades; the place where the dead go
15. A visitor in Ithaka; really Athena disguised
19. Bird often used as omen
20. One of Homer's names for the Greeks
21. Goddess who gave Odysseus her veil
22. Six-headed monster

**Down**

1. They were important to the Greeks; presents
2. Weapon of Odysseus
3. Home of the Phaikians
4. Sign of good or bad luck to come
6. God of the sea; seeks revenge on Odysseus for blinding his son
7. King of Pylos; reminisces about the good old days
10. God of the sun; owner of cattle
11. Odysseus' faithful swineherd
12. Nurse for both Odysseus & Telemakhos
13. Kyklops who captured Odysseus & his men
16. Daughter of the King of Phaikia
17. Agamemnon's son
18. Wife of Menelaus; the Prince of Troy abducted her

Odyssey Crossword 1 Answer Key

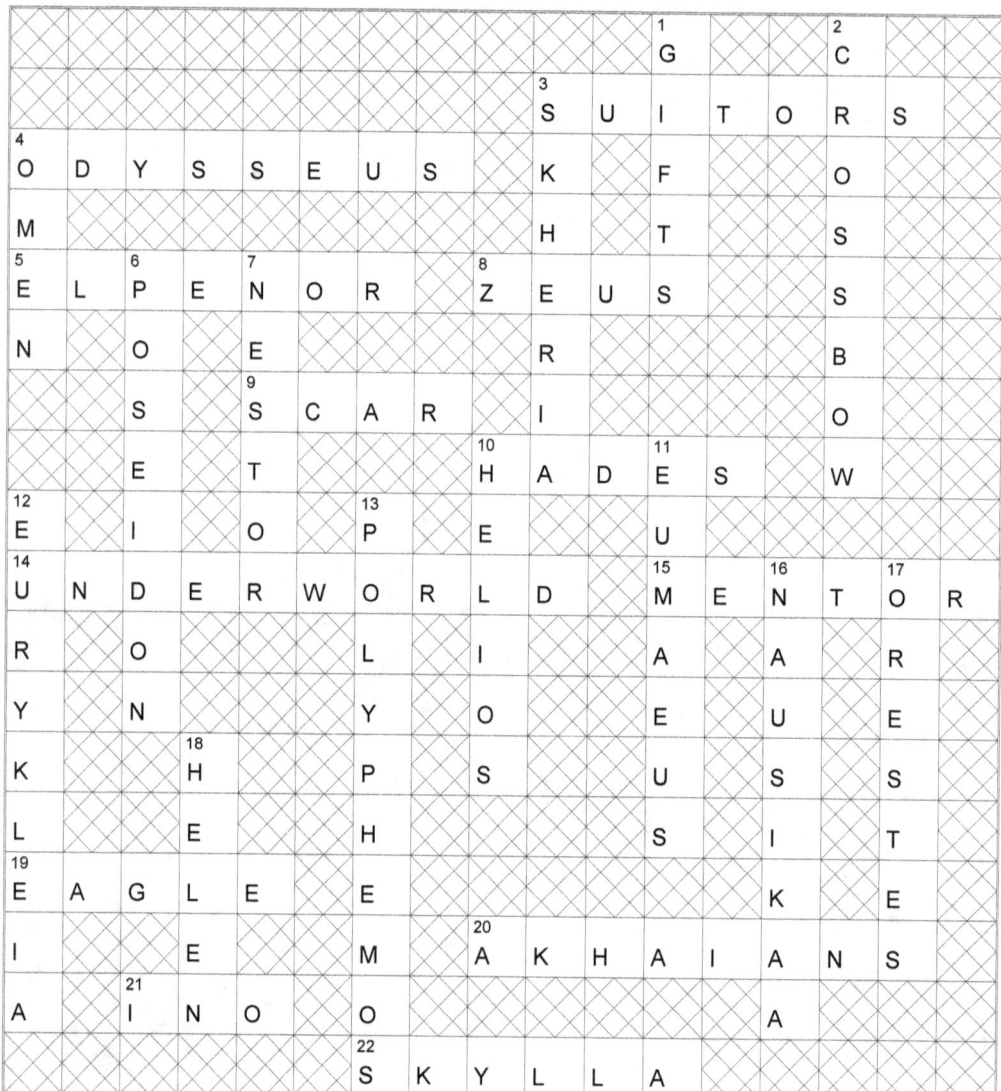

**Across**
3. The men who wanted to marry Penelope
4. Hero of the Trojan War who goes on a journey
5. One of Odysseus' crew; fell from Kirke's roof
8. King of the gods; lives on Mt. Olympus
9. Means by which which Odysseus is recognized by nurse
10. Ruler of the underworld; brother to Zeus and Poseidon
14. Guarded by Hades; the place where the dead go
15. A visitor in Ithaka; really Athena disguised
19. Bird often used as omen
20. One of Homer's names for the Greeks
21. Goddess who gave Odysseus her veil
22. Six-headed monster

**Down**
1. They were important to the Greeks; presents
2. Weapon of Odysseus
3. Home of the Phaikians
4. Sign of good or bad luck to come
6. God of the sea; seeks revenge on Odysseus for blinding his son
7. King of Pylos; reminisces about the good old days
10. God of the sun; owner of cattle
11. Odysseus' faithful swineherd
12. Nurse for both Odysseus & Telemakhos
13. Kyklops who captured Odysseus & his men
16. Daughter of the King of Phaikia
17. Agamemnon's son
18. Wife of Menelaus; the Prince of Troy abducted her

# Odyssey Crossword 2

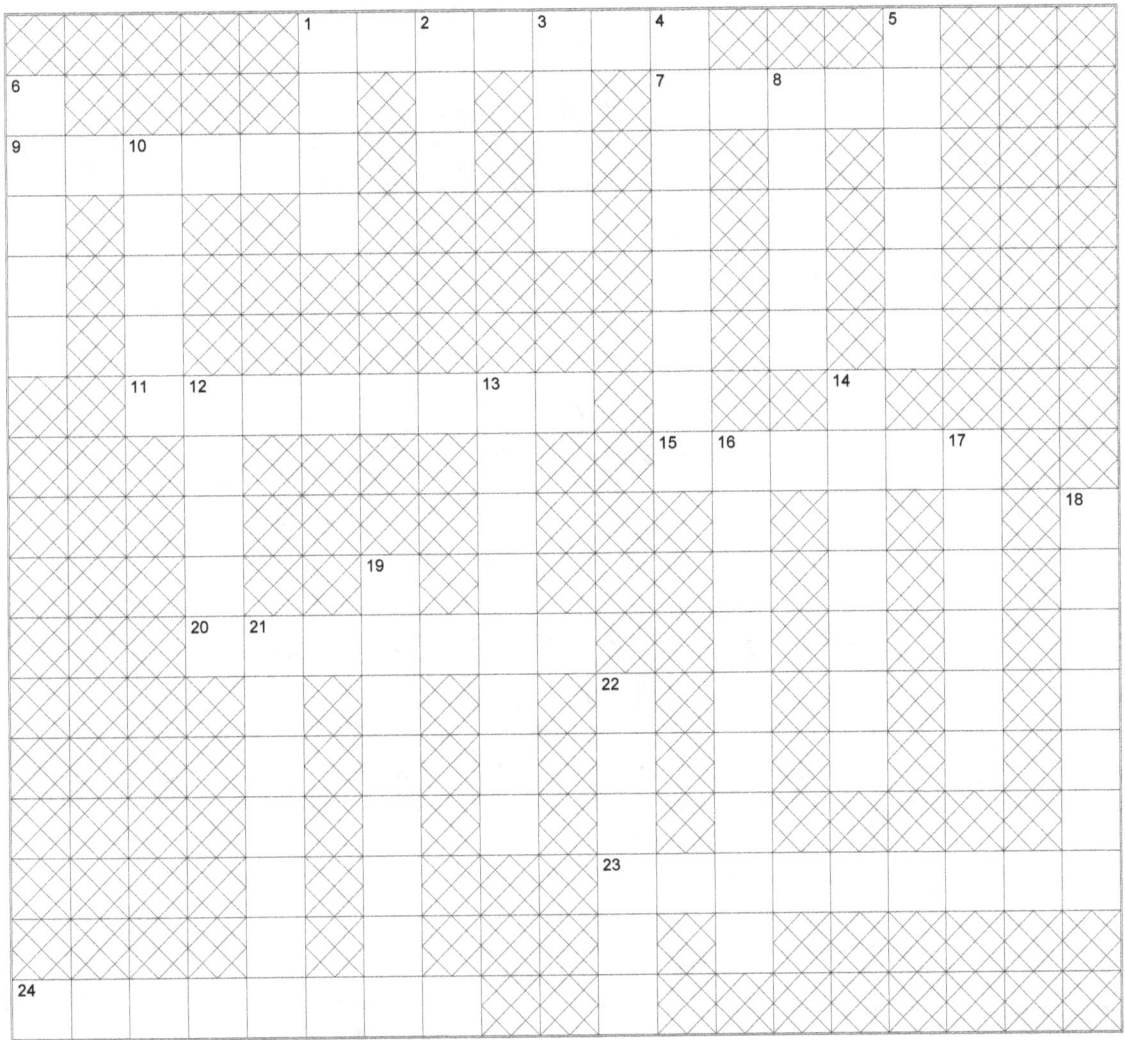

**Across**
1. The men who wanted to marry Penelope
7. Bird often used as omen
9. Native land and home of Odysseus
11. Daughter of the King of Phaikia
15. Six-headed monster
20. Home of the Phaikians
23. Blind prophet whom Odysseus visited in the underworld
24. The one-eyed giants

**Down**
1. Means by which which Odysseus is recognized by nurse
2. Goddess who gave Odysseus her veil
3. Sign of good or bad luck to come
4. Nymphs whose singing entices men to land on their island
5. A visitor in Ithaka; really Athena disguised
6. Goddess who tried to turn Odysseus & crew into pigs
8. They were important to the Greeks; presents
10. Wife of Menelaus; the Prince of Troy abducted her
12. Odysseus's dog
13. One of Homer's names for the Greeks
14. One of Odysseus' crew; fell from Kirke's roof
16. Whirlpool that sucked down ship and crewmen
17. A mortal to whom the gods have given control of the winds
18. Odysseus' faithful swineherd
19. Faithful wife of Odysseus
21. Goddess who kept Odysseus on her island for years
22. King of Pylos; reminisces about the good old days

Odyssey Crossword 2 Answer Key

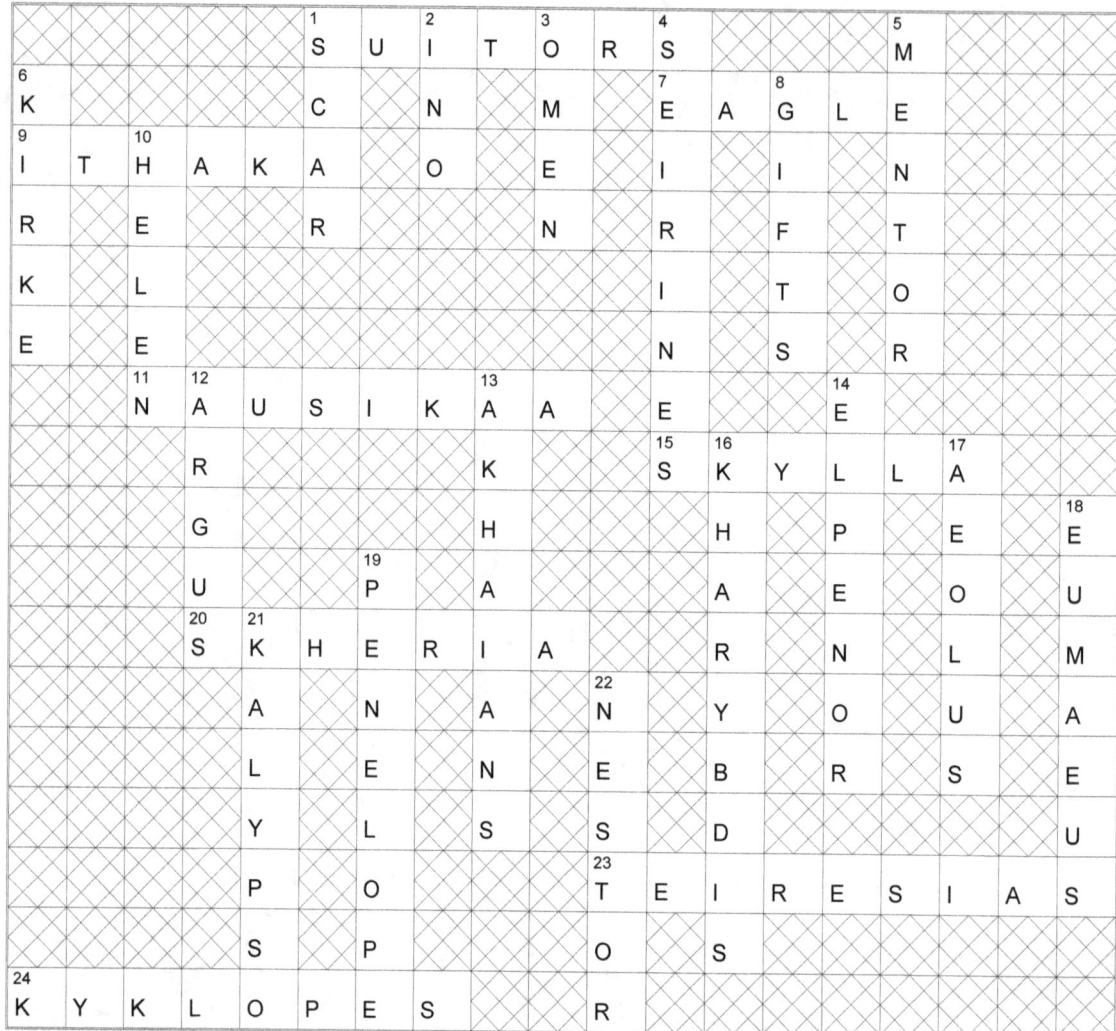

Across
1. The men who wanted to marry Penelope
7. Bird often used as omen
9. Native land and home of Odysseus
11. Daughter of the King of Phaikia
15. Six-headed monster
20. Home of the Phaikians
23. Blind prophet whom Odysseus visited in the underworld
24. The one-eyed giants

Down
1. Means by which which Odysseus is recognized by nurse
2. Goddess who gave Odysseus her veil
3. Sign of good or bad luck to come
4. Nymphs whose singing entices men to land on their island
5. A visitor in Ithaka; really Athena disguised
6. Goddess who tried to turn Odysseus & crew into pigs
8. They were important to the Greeks; presents
10. Wife of Menelaus; the Prince of Troy abducted her
12. Odysseus's dog
13. One of Homer's names for the Greeks
14. One of Odysseus' crew; fell from Kirke's roof
16. Whirlpool that sucked down ship and crewmen
17. A mortal to whom the gods have given control of the winds
18. Odysseus' faithful swineherd
19. Faithful wife of Odysseus
21. Goddess who kept Odysseus on her island for years
22. King of Pylos; reminisces about the good old days

Odyssey Crossword 3

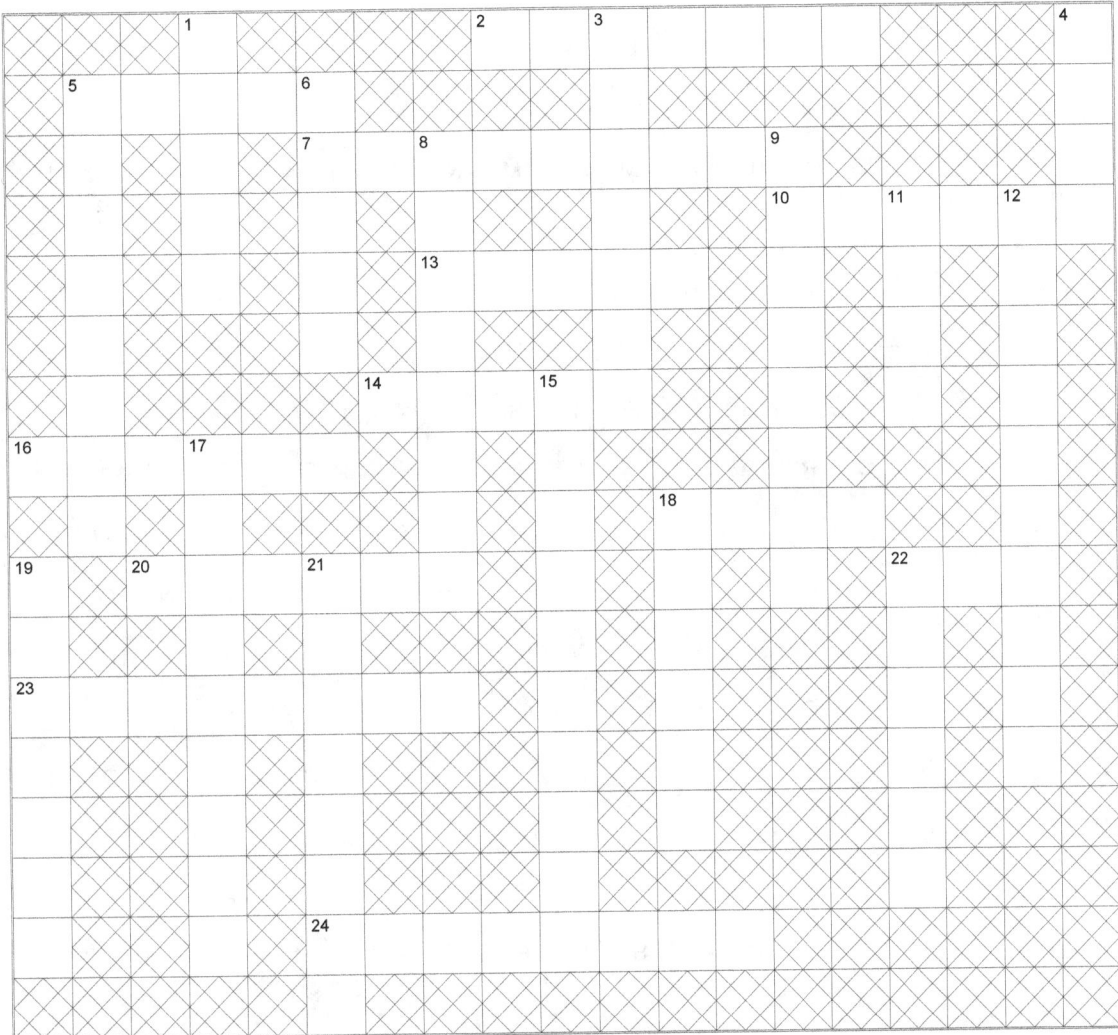

**Across**
2. Father of Odysseus
5. Goddess who tried to turn Odysseus & crew into pigs
7. King of Mycene; murdered by his wife & her lover
10. A mortal to whom the gods have given control of the winds
13. Ruler of the underworld; brother to Zeus and Poseidon
14. They were important to the Greeks; presents
16. A visitor in Ithaka; really Athena disguised
18. Means by which which Odysseus is recognized by nurse
20. Plate-like object that is thrown in contests
22. Goddess who gave Odysseus her veil
23. Faithful wife of Odysseus
24. Hero of the Trojan War who goes on a journey

**Down**
1. Odysseus's dog
3. Odysseus' faithful swineherd
4. King of the gods; lives on Mt. Olympus
5. The one-eyed giants
6. Bird often used as omen
8. One of Homer's names for the Greeks
9. Daughter of the King of Phaikia
11. Sign of good or bad luck to come
12. Guarded by Hades; the place where the dead go
15. Son of Odysseus
17. Blind prophet whom Odysseus visited in the underworld
18. Six-headed monster
19. One of Odysseus' crew; fell from Kirke's roof
21. Weapon of Odysseus
22. Native land and home of Odysseus

Odyssey Crossword 3 Answer Key

**Across**
2. Father of Odysseus
5. Goddess who tried to turn Odysseus & crew into pigs
7. King of Mycene; murdered by his wife & her lover
10. A mortal to whom the gods have given control of the winds
13. Ruler of the underworld; brother to Zeus and Poseidon
14. They were important to the Greeks; presents
16. A visitor in Ithaka; really Athena disguised
18. Means by which which Odysseus is recognized by nurse
20. Plate-like object that is thrown in contests
22. Goddess who gave Odysseus her veil
23. Faithful wife of Odysseus
24. Hero of the Trojan War who goes on a journey

**Down**
1. Odysseus's dog
3. Odysseus' faithful swineherd
4. King of the gods; lives on Mt. Olympus
5. The one-eyed giants
6. Bird often used as omen
8. One of Homer's names for the Greeks
9. Daughter of the King of Phaikia
11. Sign of good or bad luck to come
12. Guarded by Hades; the place where the dead go
15. Son of Odysseus
17. Blind prophet whom Odysseus visited in the underworld
18. Six-headed monster
19. One of Odysseus' crew; fell from Kirke's roof
21. Weapon of Odysseus
22. Native land and home of Odysseus

# Odyssey Crossword 4

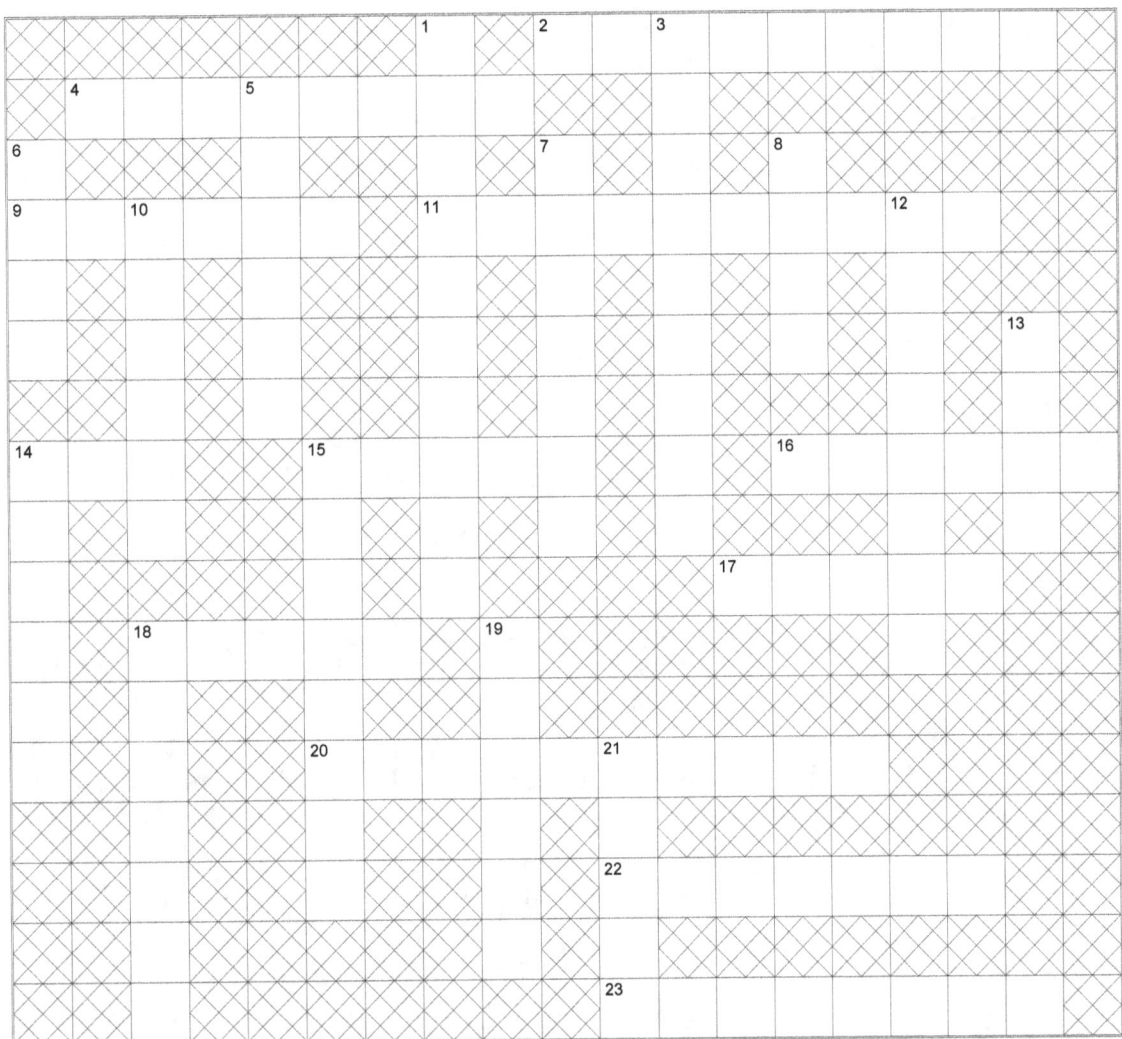

**Across**
2. Whirlpool that sucked down ship and crewmen
4. One of Homer's names for the Greeks
9. A visitor in Ithaka; really Athena disguised
11. One of the suitors; threw a stool at Odysseus
14. Goddess who gave Odysseus her veil
15. Goddess who tried to turn Odysseus & crew into pigs
16. Plate-like object that is thrown in contests
17. Odysseus's dog
18. Bird often used as omen
20. Kyklops who captured Odysseus & his men
22. Father of Odysseus
23. Daughter of the King of Phaikia

**Down**
1. Guarded by Hades; the place where the dead go
3. King of Mycene; murdered by his wife & her lover
5. A mortal to whom the gods have given control of the winds
6. Sign of good or bad luck to come
7. Agamemnon's son
8. Means by which which Odysseus is recognized by nurse
10. King of Pylos; reminisces about the good old days
12. Hero of the Trojan War who goes on a journey
13. King of the gods; lives on Mt. Olympus
14. Native land and home of Odysseus
15. The one-eyed giants
18. One of Odysseus' crew; fell from Kirke's roof
19. Six-headed monster
21. Wife of Menelaus; the Prince of Troy abducted her

Odyssey Crossword 4 Answer Key

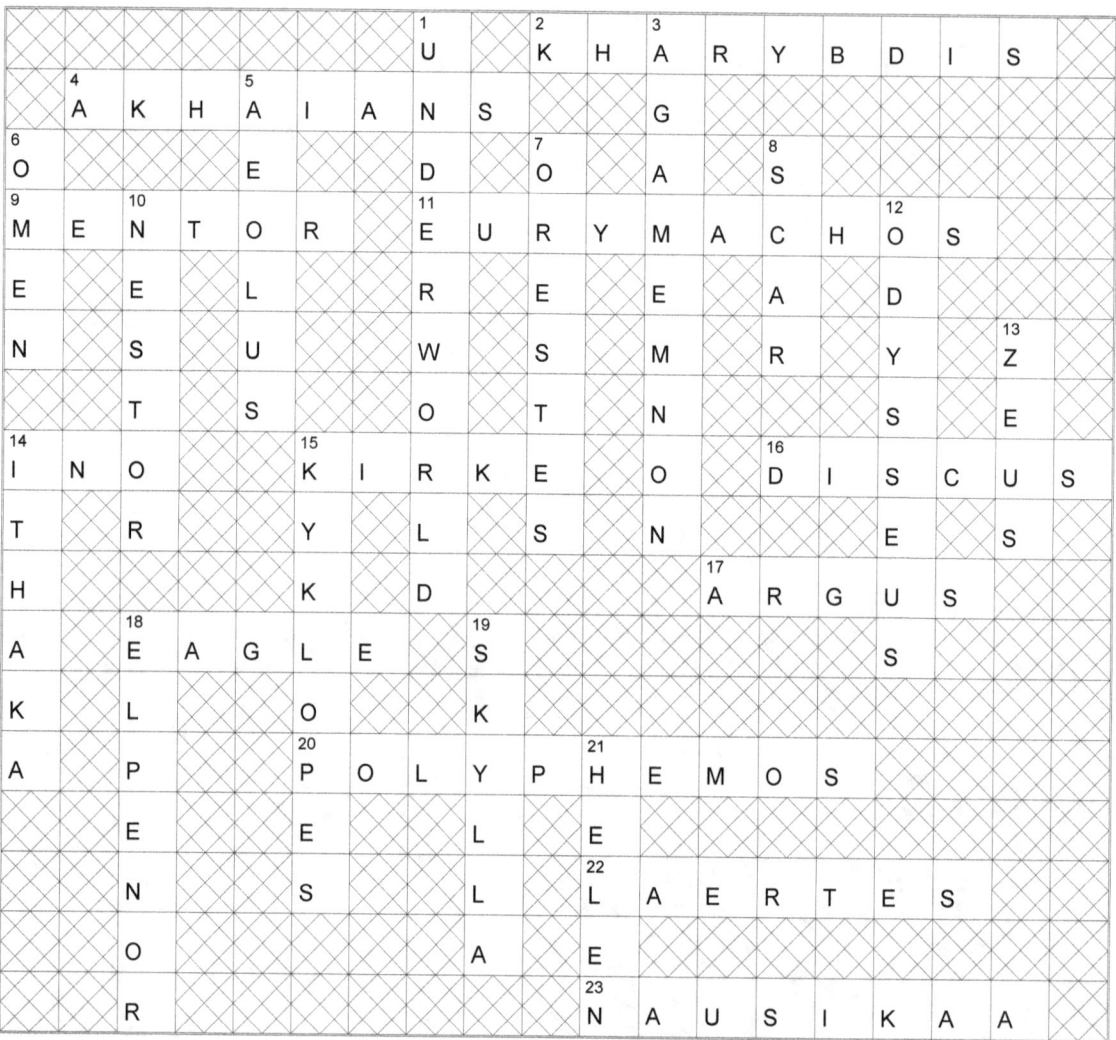

**Across**
2. Whirlpool that sucked down ship and crewmen
4. One of Homer's names for the Greeks
9. A visitor in Ithaka; really Athena disguised
11. One of the suitors; threw a stool at Odysseus
14. Goddess who gave Odysseus her veil
15. Goddess who tried to turn Odysseus & crew into pigs
16. Plate-like object that is thrown in contests
17. Odysseus's dog
18. Bird often used as omen
20. Kyklops who captured Odysseus & his men
22. Father of Odysseus
23. Daughter of the King of Phaikia

**Down**
1. Guarded by Hades; the place where the dead go
3. King of Mycene; murdered by his wife & her lover
5. A mortal to whom the gods have given control of the winds
6. Sign of good or bad luck to come
7. Agamemnon's son
8. Means by which which Odysseus is recognized by nurse
10. King of Pylos; reminisces about the good old days
12. Hero of the Trojan War who goes on a journey
13. King of the gods; lives on Mt. Olympus
14. Native land and home of Odysseus
15. The one-eyed giants
18. One of Odysseus' crew; fell from Kirke's roof
19. Six-headed monster
21. Wife of Menelaus; the Prince of Troy abducted her

Odyssey

| EUMAEUS | TEIRESIAS | ODYSSEUS | HELEN | TELEMAKHOS |
|---|---|---|---|---|
| ORESTES | ARGUS | KYKLOPES | LAESTRYGONIANS | SKYLLA |
| UNDERWORLD | EAGLE | FREE SPACE | KLYTIAMNESTRA | KHARYBDIS |
| INO | SEIRINES | LAERTES | ELPENOR | SCAR |
| POLYPHEMOS | AKHAIANS | DISCUS | ITHAKA | MENELAUS |

Odyssey

| EURYKLEIA | NAUSIKAA | SKHERIA | NESTOR | SUITORS |
|---|---|---|---|---|
| POSEIDON | ZEUS | EURYMACHOS | HADES | CROSSBOW |
| PENELOPE | HELIOS | FREE SPACE | MENTOR | GIFTS |
| OMEN | AGAMEMNON | KIRKE | MENELAUS | ITHAKA |
| DISCUS | AKHAIANS | POLYPHEMOS | SCAR | ELPENOR |

Odyssey

| EUMAEUS | KYKLOPES | LAESTRYGONIANS | EURYMACHOS | HADES |
|---|---|---|---|---|
| ARGUS | SUITORS | ORESTES | SEIRINES | MENELAUS |
| ELPENOR | TELEMAKHOS | FREE SPACE | POLYPHEMOS | POSEIDON |
| KLYTIAMNESTRA | MENTOR | NESTOR | ZEUS | DISCUS |
| KIRKE | AKHAIANS | UNDERWORLD | PENELOPE | SCAR |

Odyssey

| SKYLLA | NAUSIKAA | HELEN | ODYSSEUS | ITHAKA |
|---|---|---|---|---|
| CROSSBOW | TEIRESIAS | KALYPSO | AGAMEMNON | EAGLE |
| INO | HELIOS | FREE SPACE | LAERTES | AEOLUS |
| KHARYBDIS | EURYKLEIA | OMEN | SCAR | PENELOPE |
| UNDERWORLD | AKHAIANS | KIRKE | DISCUS | ZEUS |

## Odyssey

| NAUSIKAA | INO | KHARYBDIS | KALYPSO | KLYTIAMNESTRA |
|---|---|---|---|---|
| SEIRINES | HADES | LAERTES | MENTOR | ARGUS |
| AGAMEMNON | HELEN | FREE SPACE | ODYSSEUS | ZEUS |
| KIRKE | DISCUS | TEIRESIAS | SKYLLA | POLYPHEMOS |
| AEOLUS | KYKLOPES | POSEIDON | EUMAEUS | PENELOPE |

## Odyssey

| ORESTES | SUITORS | CROSSBOW | SCAR | ITHAKA |
|---|---|---|---|---|
| EAGLE | UNDERWORLD | ELPENOR | TELEMAKHOS | SKHERIA |
| EURYKLEIA | GIFTS | FREE SPACE | EURYMACHOS | OMEN |
| NESTOR | LAESTRYGONIANS | HELIOS | PENELOPE | EUMAEUS |
| POSEIDON | KYKLOPES | AEOLUS | POLYPHEMOS | SKYLLA |

Odyssey

| EAGLE | UNDERWORLD | KALYPSO | SKYLLA | OMEN |
|---|---|---|---|---|
| HELIOS | KYKLOPES | KLYTIAMNESTRA | TELEMAKHOS | HELEN |
| SCAR | PENELOPE | FREE SPACE | ZEUS | SKHERIA |
| CROSSBOW | EUMAEUS | GIFTS | ARGUS | AKHAIANS |
| EURYMACHOS | KHARYBDIS | MENTOR | ODYSSEUS | KIRKE |

Odyssey

| POLYPHEMOS | AEOLUS | LAERTES | AGAMEMNON | HADES |
|---|---|---|---|---|
| EURYKLEIA | LAESTRYGONIANS | ORESTES | SUITORS | NESTOR |
| INO | ELPENOR | FREE SPACE | NAUSIKAA | DISCUS |
| POSEIDON | ITHAKA | TEIRESIAS | KIRKE | ODYSSEUS |
| MENTOR | KHARYBDIS | EURYMACHOS | AKHAIANS | ARGUS |

Odyssey

| KHARYBDIS | GIFTS | KYKLOPES | MENELAUS | AKHAIANS |
|---|---|---|---|---|
| POSEIDON | LAESTRYGONIANS | ITHAKA | DISCUS | TELEMAKHOS |
| NESTOR | AGAMEMNON | FREE SPACE | SUITORS | ZEUS |
| KALYPSO | EURYKLEIA | EAGLE | ODYSSEUS | TEIRESIAS |
| ARGUS | EURYMACHOS | HELEN | SCAR | ORESTES |

Odyssey

| UNDERWORLD | LAERTES | INO | SKHERIA | SEIRINES |
|---|---|---|---|---|
| PENELOPE | POLYPHEMOS | HADES | CROSSBOW | SKYLLA |
| NAUSIKAA | KIRKE | FREE SPACE | ELPENOR | MENTOR |
| KLYTIAMNESTRA | OMEN | EUMAEUS | ORESTES | SCAR |
| HELEN | EURYMACHOS | ARGUS | TEIRESIAS | ODYSSEUS |

Odyssey

| | | | | |
|---|---|---|---|---|
| OMEN | UNDERWORLD | TEIRESIAS | CROSSBOW | HELIOS |
| KLYTIAMNESTRA | LAERTES | EAGLE | ELPENOR | KALYPSO |
| SCAR | HELEN | FREE SPACE | TELEMAKHOS | ITHAKA |
| AEOLUS | NESTOR | PENELOPE | AKHAIANS | POLYPHEMOS |
| KHARYBDIS | INO | GIFTS | EURYKLEIA | KYKLOPES |

Odyssey

| | | | | |
|---|---|---|---|---|
| MENELAUS | MENTOR | POSEIDON | LAESTRYGONIANS | NAUSIKAA |
| EURYMACHOS | KIRKE | SEIRINES | SKHERIA | ZEUS |
| DISCUS | AGAMEMNON | FREE SPACE | HADES | ORESTES |
| SKYLLA | ARGUS | SUITORS | KYKLOPES | EURYKLEIA |
| GIFTS | INO | KHARYBDIS | POLYPHEMOS | AKHAIANS |

## Odyssey

| HELEN | CROSSBOW | AEOLUS | TELEMAKHOS | POLYPHEMOS |
|---|---|---|---|---|
| HELIOS | NESTOR | ARGUS | MENELAUS | PENELOPE |
| KLYTIAMNESTRA | AKHAIANS | FREE SPACE | SEIRINES | OMEN |
| ELPENOR | SKYLLA | SKHERIA | EURYKLEIA | TEIRESIAS |
| EUMAEUS | KIRKE | POSEIDON | ODYSSEUS | SCAR |

## Odyssey

| MENTOR | INO | KALYPSO | ITHAKA | ZEUS |
|---|---|---|---|---|
| KHARYBDIS | KYKLOPES | SUITORS | GIFTS | AGAMEMNON |
| UNDERWORLD | NAUSIKAA | FREE SPACE | DISCUS | EURYMACHOS |
| LAERTES | ORESTES | LAESTRYGONIANS | SCAR | ODYSSEUS |
| POSEIDON | KIRKE | EUMAEUS | TEIRESIAS | EURYKLEIA |

Odyssey

| OMEN | AKHAIANS | ZEUS | ODYSSEUS | TEIRESIAS |
|---|---|---|---|---|
| SKYLLA | TELEMAKHOS | KLYTIAMNESTRA | EUMAEUS | DISCUS |
| SUITORS | HELEN | FREE SPACE | PENELOPE | ITHAKA |
| CROSSBOW | SEIRINES | KHARYBDIS | GIFTS | POSEIDON |
| LAESTRYGONIANS | EURYMACHOS | EURYKLEIA | EAGLE | POLYPHEMOS |

Odyssey

| SCAR | HELIOS | KALYPSO | MENELAUS | LAERTES |
|---|---|---|---|---|
| SKHERIA | NESTOR | ARGUS | INO | NAUSIKAA |
| ORESTES | KYKLOPES | FREE SPACE | HADES | AEOLUS |
| AGAMEMNON | KIRKE | MENTOR | POLYPHEMOS | EAGLE |
| EURYKLEIA | EURYMACHOS | LAESTRYGONIANS | POSEIDON | GIFTS |

Odyssey

| | | | | |
|---|---|---|---|---|
| EAGLE | SKYLLA | KHARYBDIS | LAERTES | EUMAEUS |
| KALYPSO | CROSSBOW | OMEN | ODYSSEUS | TEIRESIAS |
| EURYKLEIA | MENTOR | FREE SPACE | KYKLOPES | KIRKE |
| EURYMACHOS | AEOLUS | POSEIDON | SKHERIA | UNDERWORLD |
| ZEUS | MENELAUS | ORESTES | SCAR | ARGUS |

Odyssey

| | | | | |
|---|---|---|---|---|
| INO | SUITORS | HELEN | HADES | AKHAIANS |
| POLYPHEMOS | NESTOR | LAESTRYGONIANS | ITHAKA | DISCUS |
| AGAMEMNON | HELIOS | FREE SPACE | ELPENOR | GIFTS |
| PENELOPE | KLYTIAMNESTRA | TELEMAKHOS | ARGUS | SCAR |
| ORESTES | MENELAUS | ZEUS | UNDERWORLD | SKHERIA |

Odyssey

| EURYKLEIA | UNDERWORLD | EUMAEUS | SUITORS | NESTOR |
|---|---|---|---|---|
| INO | TEIRESIAS | SKYLLA | SEIRINES | ARGUS |
| OMEN | LAESTRYGONIANS | FREE SPACE | KLYTIAMNESTRA | ORESTES |
| AKHAIANS | KIRKE | ODYSSEUS | SKHERIA | KHARYBDIS |
| POSEIDON | TELEMAKHOS | ELPENOR | MENTOR | LAERTES |

Odyssey

| EAGLE | DISCUS | EURYMACHOS | MENELAUS | HELIOS |
|---|---|---|---|---|
| KALYPSO | ITHAKA | PENELOPE | POLYPHEMOS | KYKLOPES |
| SCAR | HADES | FREE SPACE | GIFTS | HELEN |
| AEOLUS | ZEUS | CROSSBOW | LAERTES | MENTOR |
| ELPENOR | TELEMAKHOS | POSEIDON | KHARYBDIS | SKHERIA |

## Odyssey

| | | | | |
|---|---|---|---|---|
| HADES | ELPENOR | EAGLE | POLYPHEMOS | ARGUS |
| KYKLOPES | ODYSSEUS | TELEMAKHOS | LAESTRYGONIANS | EURYKLEIA |
| KLYTIAMNESTRA | CROSSBOW | FREE SPACE | KALYPSO | MENELAUS |
| ITHAKA | PENELOPE | HELIOS | SCAR | INO |
| UNDERWORLD | POSEIDON | DISCUS | TEIRESIAS | EUMAEUS |

## Odyssey

| | | | | |
|---|---|---|---|---|
| SUITORS | LAERTES | NESTOR | AEOLUS | KHARYBDIS |
| EURYMACHOS | KIRKE | SKYLLA | ZEUS | GIFTS |
| AGAMEMNON | MENTOR | FREE SPACE | AKHAIANS | OMEN |
| ORESTES | SKHERIA | HELEN | EUMAEUS | TEIRESIAS |
| DISCUS | POSEIDON | UNDERWORLD | INO | SCAR |

## Odyssey

| | | | | |
|---|---|---|---|---|
| KYKLOPES | ODYSSEUS | TELEMAKHOS | HADES | EUMAEUS |
| ELPENOR | MENTOR | ZEUS | AGAMEMNON | NAUSIKAA |
| ITHAKA | INO | FREE SPACE | NESTOR | ORESTES |
| OMEN | AKHAIANS | KHARYBDIS | PENELOPE | SEIRINES |
| EURYMACHOS | HELIOS | ARGUS | SUITORS | SKHERIA |

## Odyssey

| | | | | |
|---|---|---|---|---|
| EURYKLEIA | KIRKE | DISCUS | UNDERWORLD | POSEIDON |
| CROSSBOW | LAERTES | KALYPSO | GIFTS | HELEN |
| TEIRESIAS | SCAR | FREE SPACE | KLYTIAMNESTRA | POLYPHEMOS |
| AEOLUS | SKYLLA | LAESTRYGONIANS | SKHERIA | SUITORS |
| ARGUS | HELIOS | EURYMACHOS | SEIRINES | PENELOPE |

Odyssey

| | | | | |
|---|---|---|---|---|
| INO | GIFTS | TELEMAKHOS | DISCUS | POLYPHEMOS |
| SKYLLA | EURYKLEIA | AGAMEMNON | KHARYBDIS | ORESTES |
| KALYPSO | ODYSSEUS | FREE SPACE | HADES | SUITORS |
| AEOLUS | LAERTES | SCAR | ARGUS | MENTOR |
| EAGLE | ITHAKA | ZEUS | KIRKE | AKHAIANS |

Odyssey

| | | | | |
|---|---|---|---|---|
| HELIOS | KYKLOPES | HELEN | KLYTIAMNESTRA | CROSSBOW |
| NESTOR | ELPENOR | SKHERIA | OMEN | UNDERWORLD |
| EUMAEUS | TEIRESIAS | FREE SPACE | LAESTRYGONIANS | NAUSIKAA |
| POSEIDON | EURYMACHOS | MENELAUS | AKHAIANS | KIRKE |
| ZEUS | ITHAKA | EAGLE | MENTOR | ARGUS |

Odyssey

| NAUSIKAA | SCAR | ODYSSEUS | INO | ITHAKA |
|---|---|---|---|---|
| KHARYBDIS | EUMAEUS | MENTOR | AEOLUS | EURYKLEIA |
| ARGUS | SEIRINES | FREE SPACE | HELIOS | EURYMACHOS |
| POSEIDON | ZEUS | OMEN | SUITORS | MENELAUS |
| LAERTES | EAGLE | POLYPHEMOS | SKHERIA | NESTOR |

Odyssey

| HELEN | KYKLOPES | SKYLLA | PENELOPE | DISCUS |
|---|---|---|---|---|
| TELEMAKHOS | HADES | KIRKE | AKHAIANS | TEIRESIAS |
| KLYTIAMNESTRA | CROSSBOW | FREE SPACE | AGAMEMNON | ORESTES |
| ELPENOR | GIFTS | KALYPSO | NESTOR | SKHERIA |
| POLYPHEMOS | EAGLE | LAERTES | MENELAUS | SUITORS |

## Odyssey

| NAUSIKAA | EURYKLEIA | ARGUS | AKHAIANS | HADES |
|---|---|---|---|---|
| OMEN | HELEN | EURYMACHOS | SKHERIA | LAESTRYGONIANS |
| SEIRINES | LAERTES | FREE SPACE | POLYPHEMOS | KHARYBDIS |
| KALYPSO | INO | AGAMEMNON | POSEIDON | EAGLE |
| HELIOS | DISCUS | MENELAUS | KYKLOPES | SKYLLA |

## Odyssey

| ODYSSEUS | GIFTS | CROSSBOW | SCAR | TEIRESIAS |
|---|---|---|---|---|
| KLYTIAMNESTRA | ITHAKA | EUMAEUS | MENTOR | KIRKE |
| AEOLUS | SUITORS | FREE SPACE | ORESTES | ZEUS |
| NESTOR | ELPENOR | PENELOPE | SKYLLA | KYKLOPES |
| MENELAUS | DISCUS | HELIOS | EAGLE | POSEIDON |

Odyssey

| DISCUS | CROSSBOW | MENELAUS | SCAR | EAGLE |
|---|---|---|---|---|
| KALYPSO | AGAMEMNON | KYKLOPES | HELEN | AEOLUS |
| KIRKE | SKYLLA | FREE SPACE | EURYKLEIA | POLYPHEMOS |
| SEIRINES | EUMAEUS | ODYSSEUS | ITHAKA | UNDERWORLD |
| SKHERIA | INO | LAERTES | TEIRESIAS | EURYMACHOS |

Odyssey

| OMEN | ARGUS | AKHAIANS | ORESTES | TELEMAKHOS |
|---|---|---|---|---|
| LAESTRYGONIANS | NAUSIKAA | SUITORS | ELPENOR | POSEIDON |
| MENTOR | ZEUS | FREE SPACE | KHARYBDIS | HADES |
| HELIOS | NESTOR | KLYTIAMNESTRA | EURYMACHOS | TEIRESIAS |
| LAERTES | INO | SKHERIA | UNDERWORLD | ITHAKA |

## Odyssey Vocabulary Word List

| No. | Word | Clue/Definition |
|---|---|---|
| 1. | ADZE | Axe-like tool with arched blade at right angles to the handle |
| 2. | ANNIHILATION | The act of destroying completely |
| 3. | ANODYNE | Anything that soothes or confronts |
| 4. | APPALLED | Filled with dismay |
| 5. | ARROGANCE | Insolent pride |
| 6. | AUDACITY | Boldness or daring |
| 7. | AUGURY | Interpreting signs and omens |
| 8. | AUSPICIOUS | Attended to by favorable circumstances |
| 9. | BALSAM | Tree that yields an aromatic, sticky substance |
| 10. | BENEVOLENT | Kind |
| 11. | BIER | Stand on which a coffin or corpse is placed |
| 12. | BILGE | Water that collects in the low part of a ship's hull |
| 13. | BRACE | A pair |
| 14. | BRUTAL | Cruel or harsh |
| 15. | CACHE | Hole or hiding place |
| 16. | CALAMITOUS | Causing or involving a disaster |
| 17. | CANDOR | Frankness; sincerity |
| 18. | CHATTELS | Articles of personal, movable property; slaves |
| 19. | CLARION | Shrill and clear |
| 20. | CLEFT | Division, separation |
| 21. | CODDLED | Treated indulgently; babied |
| 22. | COLLOQUY | Formal conversation |
| 23. | COLONNADE | Series of columns placed at regular intervals |
| 24. | COMELY | Attractive; handsome; graceful |
| 25. | COMPUNCTION | Strong uneasiness caused by a sense of guilt |
| 26. | CONTENDING | Striving in battle or controversy |
| 27. | CONTENTIOUSLY | In a quarrelsome way |
| 28. | CORSAIRS | Pirates |
| 29. | CRANING | Stretching and straining |
| 30. | DEFERENCE | Courteous respect |
| 31. | DERELICT | Vagrant or social outcast |
| 32. | DESOLATE | Deserted; dreary, gloomy |
| 33. | DISPERSED | Scattered in different directions |
| 34. | DISSIMULATION | Concealing or disguising |
| 35. | DISTAFF | Stick on a spinning wheel that holds unspun wool |
| 36. | DOLE | Distribute in small portions |
| 37. | FARCE | Empty show; mockery |
| 38. | FEIGN | Pretend |
| 39. | FETTLE | Proper or sound condition; good spirits |
| 40. | FLOUT | Show contempt or scorn |
| 41. | GUILE | Craftiness |
| 42. | HALYARDS | Ropes used to raise or lower a sail or flag |
| 43. | HAPLESS | Luckless; unfortunate |
| 44. | HARANGUED | Delivered a long, strong-feeling speech |
| 45. | HOVERED | Floated as if suspended |
| 46. | IMPLACABLE | Incapable of being pleased |
| 47. | INTAGLIO | Design incised beneath the surface of metal |
| 48. | LIBATION | Liquid offering as a part of a religious ritual; intoxicating liquid |
| 49. | LOB | Hit, toss, or propel in a high arc |
| 50. | LUMINOUS | Emitting self-generated light |
| 51. | MEAGER | Small in quantity, fullness, or extent |

**Odyssey Vocabulary Word List Continued**

| No. | Word | Clue/Definition |
|---|---|---|
| 52. | MINIONS | Employees or domestic servants |
| 53. | MORTIFIED | Shamed or humiliated |
| 54. | MUSTER | Assemble or gather together |
| 55. | MUTINOUS | Rebellious |
| 56. | OBLIVION | State of being completely forgotten |
| 57. | OBSTINACY | Stubbornness |
| 58. | ORDAINED | Prearranged; predestined |
| 59. | PATRIMONY | Inheritance from a father |
| 60. | PERPLEXITY | State of being puzzled or confused |
| 61. | PETRELS | Sea birds |
| 62. | PITH | Essential or central part of anything |
| 63. | PLUNDERED | Robbed of goods by force |
| 64. | PRECEDENCE | Priority; going in advance |
| 65. | PREVAILS | Triumphs or wins |
| 66. | PRODIGIOUS | Impressively great in size |
| 67. | PROFUSION | Abundance; extravagance |
| 68. | PROMONTORY | High ridge of land or rock jutting into the sea |
| 69. | PROWESS | Superior skill or ability |
| 70. | PUNGENT | A sharp, bitter taste |
| 71. | RANCOR | Bitter, long-lasting resentment |
| 72. | REBUKE | Criticize sharply |
| 73. | RESPLENDENT | Brilliant |
| 74. | RETAINER | Subordinates of an organization or an individual |
| 75. | SAURIAN | Lizard-like |
| 76. | SCORE | Group of twenty items |
| 77. | STALWART | Having physical strength |
| 78. | STEEPED | Soaked |
| 79. | STINTED | Restricted or limited |
| 80. | SUCCUMBED | Yielded or submitted to an overpowering force |
| 81. | SUPPLICATION | Plea; asking for humbly or earnestly |
| 82. | SURMISED | Inferred without conclusive evidence; guessed; gathered |
| 83. | TACTICIAN | A person skilled in maneuvering |
| 84. | TAUT | Pulled or drawn tight |
| 85. | TIMOROUS | Apprehensive; fearfully cautious |
| 86. | TUMULT | Disorderly commotion |
| 87. | TYRO | Beginner or inexperienced person |
| 88. | VALOR | Courage and boldness |
| 89. | VAUNT | Boast or brag |
| 90. | VIE | To compete or strive for victory |
| 91. | VIGILANCE | Watchfulness |
| 92. | VIVACITY | Liveliness |
| 93. | WANED | Approached an end |
| 94. | WIELDING | Handling a weapon or a tool |
| 95. | WINDFALL | Sudden and unexpected piece of good fortune |

Copyrighted

Odyssey Vocabulary Fill In The Blank 1

_____

_____

_____

_____

_____

_____

_____

_____

_____

_____

_____

_____

_____

_____

_____

_____

_____

_____

_____

_____

1. Striving in battle or controversy
2. Insolent pride
3. Hole or hiding place
4. Articles of personal, movable property; slaves
5. Watchfulness
6. In a quarrelsome way
7. Tree that yields an aromatic, sticky substance
8. Beginner or inexperienced person
9. Courage and boldness
10. Superior skill or ability
11. A pair
12. Attended to by favorable circumstances
13. Brilliant
14. Concealing or disguising
15. Hit, toss, or propel in a high arc
16. High ridge of land or rock jutting into the sea
17. Having physical strength
18. Ropes used to raise or lower a sail or flag
19. Craftiness
20. Cruel or harsh

Odyssey Vocabulary Fill In The Blank 1 Answer Key

| CONTENDING | 1. Striving in battle or controversy |
| ARROGANCE | 2. Insolent pride |
| CACHE | 3. Hole or hiding place |
| CHATTELS | 4. Articles of personal, movable property; slaves |
| VIGILANCE | 5. Watchfulness |
| CONTENTIOUSLY | 6. In a quarrelsome way |
| BALSAM | 7. Tree that yields an aromatic, sticky substance |
| TYRO | 8. Beginner or inexperienced person |
| VALOR | 9. Courage and boldness |
| PROWESS | 10. Superior skill or ability |
| BRACE | 11. A pair |
| AUSPICIOUS | 12. Attended to by favorable circumstances |
| RESPLENDENT | 13. Brilliant |
| DISSIMULATION | 14. Concealing or disguising |
| LOB | 15. Hit, toss, or propel in a high arc |
| PROMONTORY | 16. High ridge of land or rock jutting into the sea |
| STALWART | 17. Having physical strength |
| HALYARDS | 18. Ropes used to raise or lower a sail or flag |
| GUILE | 19. Craftiness |
| BRUTAL | 20. Cruel or harsh |

Odyssey Vocabulary Fill In The Blank 2

_____  1. A pair

_____  2. Plea; asking for humbly or earnestly

_____  3. Brilliant

_____  4. Proper or sound condition; good spirits

_____  5. Restricted or limited

_____  6. Liveliness

_____  7. Frankness; sincerity

_____  8. Abundance; extravagance

_____  9. Hit, toss, or propel in a high arc

_____  10. Pirates

_____  11. Articles of personal, movable property; slaves

_____  12. Anything that soothes or confronts

_____  13. Floated as if suspended

_____  14. Tree that yields an aromatic, sticky substance

_____  15. Pretend

_____  16. Apprehensive; fearfully cautious

_____  17. Pulled or drawn tight

_____  18. Watchfulness

_____  19. Craftiness

_____  20. High ridge of land or rock jutting into the sea

Odyssey Vocabulary Fill In The Blank 2 Answer Key

| | |
|---|---|
| BRACE | 1. A pair |
| SUPPLICATION | 2. Plea; asking for humbly or earnestly |
| RESPLENDENT | 3. Brilliant |
| FETTLE | 4. Proper or sound condition; good spirits |
| STINTED | 5. Restricted or limited |
| VIVACITY | 6. Liveliness |
| CANDOR | 7. Frankness; sincerity |
| PROFUSION | 8. Abundance; extravagance |
| LOB | 9. Hit, toss, or propel in a high arc |
| CORSAIRS | 10. Pirates |
| CHATTELS | 11. Articles of personal, movable property; slaves |
| ANODYNE | 12. Anything that soothes or confronts |
| HOVERED | 13. Floated as if suspended |
| BALSAM | 14. Tree that yields an aromatic, sticky substance |
| FEIGN | 15. Pretend |
| TIMOROUS | 16. Apprehensive; fearfully cautious |
| TAUT | 17. Pulled or drawn tight |
| VIGILANCE | 18. Watchfulness |
| GUILE | 19. Craftiness |
| PROMONTORY | 20. High ridge of land or rock jutting into the sea |

Odyssey Vocabulary Fill In The Blank 3

_____  1. Emitting self-generated light

_____  2. Shrill and clear

_____  3. Abundance; extravagance

_____  4. Stretching and straining

_____  5. Brilliant

_____  6. Axe-like tool with arched blade at right angles to the handle

_____  7. Disorderly commotion

_____  8. Water that collects in the low part of a ship's hull

_____  9. Superior skill or ability

_____  10. Pirates

_____  11. Articles of personal, movable property; slaves

_____  12. Interpreting signs and omens

_____  13. Stubbornness

_____  14. Frankness; sincerity

_____  15. Striving in battle or controversy

_____  16. Proper or sound condition; good spirits

_____  17. Criticize sharply

_____  18. Essential or central part of anything

_____  19. Bitter, long-lasting resentment

_____  20. Incapable of being pleased

Odyssey Vocabulary Fill In The Blank 3 Answer Key

| | |
|---|---|
| LUMINOUS | 1. Emitting self-generated light |
| CLARION | 2. Shrill and clear |
| PROFUSION | 3. Abundance; extravagance |
| CRANING | 4. Stretching and straining |
| RESPLENDENT | 5. Brilliant |
| ADZE | 6. Axe-like tool with arched blade at right angles to the handle |
| TUMULT | 7. Disorderly commotion |
| BILGE | 8. Water that collects in the low part of a ship's hull |
| PROWESS | 9. Superior skill or ability |
| CORSAIRS | 10. Pirates |
| CHATTELS | 11. Articles of personal, movable property; slaves |
| AUGURY | 12. Interpreting signs and omens |
| OBSTINACY | 13. Stubbornness |
| CANDOR | 14. Frankness; sincerity |
| CONTENDING | 15. Striving in battle or controversy |
| FETTLE | 16. Proper or sound condition; good spirits |
| REBUKE | 17. Criticize sharply |
| PITH | 18. Essential or central part of anything |
| RANCOR | 19. Bitter, long-lasting resentment |
| IMPLACABLE | 20. Incapable of being pleased |

Odyssey Vocabulary Fill In The Blank 4

_____

1. Subordinates of an organization or an individual
2. Insolent pride
3. Kind
4. Concealing or disguising
5. Shamed or humiliated
6. Stretching and straining
7. Soaked
8. Water that collects in the low part of a ship's hull
9. Causing or involving a disaster
10. Employees or domestic servants
11. To compete or strive for victory
12. Interpreting signs and omens
13. Brilliant
14. Vagrant or social outcast
15. State of being completely forgotten
16. Having physical strength
17. Handling a weapon or a tool
18. Pretend
19. Sea birds
20. Beginner or inexperienced person

Odyssey Vocabulary Fill In The Blank 4 Answer Key

| | |
|---|---|
| RETAINER | 1. Subordinates of an organization or an individual |
| ARROGANCE | 2. Insolent pride |
| BENEVOLENT | 3. Kind |
| DISSIMULATION | 4. Concealing or disguising |
| MORTIFIED | 5. Shamed or humiliated |
| CRANING | 6. Stretching and straining |
| STEEPED | 7. Soaked |
| BILGE | 8. Water that collects in the low part of a ship's hull |
| CALAMITOUS | 9. Causing or involving a disaster |
| MINIONS | 10. Employees or domestic servants |
| VIE | 11. To compete or strive for victory |
| AUGURY | 12. Interpreting signs and omens |
| RESPLENDENT | 13. Brilliant |
| DERELICT | 14. Vagrant or social outcast |
| OBLIVION | 15. State of being completely forgotten |
| STALWART | 16. Having physical strength |
| WIELDING | 17. Handling a weapon or a tool |
| FEIGN | 18. Pretend |
| PETRELS | 19. Sea birds |
| TYRO | 20. Beginner or inexperienced person |

Odyssey Vocabulary  Matching 1

___ 1. HALYARDS              A. Liveliness
___ 2. SAURIAN               B. Hole or hiding place
___ 3. CHATTELS              C. Bitter, long-lasting resentment
___ 4. GUILE                 D. To compete or strive for victory
___ 5. OBSTINACY             E. Show contempt or scorn
___ 6. MUSTER                F. A person skilled in maneuvering
___ 7. TACTICIAN             G. Luckless; unfortunate
___ 8. PATRIMONY             H. Priority; going in advance
___ 9. MUTINOUS              I. In a quarrelsome way
___10. FEIGN                 J. Apprehensive; fearfully cautious
___11. PRECEDENCE            K. Boast or brag
___12. MORTIFIED             L. High ridge of land or rock jutting into the sea
___13. VAUNT                 M. Stubbornness
___14. CACHE                 N. Stretching and straining
___15. FLOUT                 O. Articles of personal, movable property; slaves
___16. VIE                   P. Craftiness
___17. CONTENTIOUSLY         Q. Assemble or gather together
___18. CRANING               R. Shamed or humiliated
___19. REBUKE                S. Pretend
___20. HAPLESS               T. Ropes used to raise or lower a sail or flag
___21. RANCOR                U. Inheritance from a father
___22. TIMOROUS              V. Cruel or harsh
___23. PROMONTORY            W. Criticize sharply
___24. BRUTAL                X. Lizard-like
___25. VIVACITY              Y. Rebellious

Odyssey Vocabulary Matching 1 Answer Key

| | | |
|---|---|---|
| T - 1. HALYARDS | | A. Liveliness |
| X - 2. SAURIAN | | B. Hole or hiding place |
| O - 3. CHATTELS | | C. Bitter, long-lasting resentment |
| P - 4. GUILE | | D. To compete or strive for victory |
| M - 5. OBSTINACY | | E. Show contempt or scorn |
| Q - 6. MUSTER | | F. A person skilled in maneuvering |
| F - 7. TACTICIAN | | G. Luckless; unfortunate |
| U - 8. PATRIMONY | | H. Priority; going in advance |
| Y - 9. MUTINOUS | | I. In a quarrelsome way |
| S - 10. FEIGN | | J. Apprehensive; fearfully cautious |
| H - 11. PRECEDENCE | | K. Boast or brag |
| R - 12. MORTIFIED | | L. High ridge of land or rock jutting into the sea |
| K - 13. VAUNT | | M. Stubbornness |
| B - 14. CACHE | | N. Stretching and straining |
| E - 15. FLOUT | | O. Articles of personal, movable property; slaves |
| D - 16. VIE | | P. Craftiness |
| I - 17. CONTENTIOUSLY | | Q. Assemble or gather together |
| N - 18. CRANING | | R. Shamed or humiliated |
| W - 19. REBUKE | | S. Pretend |
| G - 20. HAPLESS | | T. Ropes used to raise or lower a sail or flag |
| C - 21. RANCOR | | U. Inheritance from a father |
| J - 22. TIMOROUS | | V. Cruel or harsh |
| L - 23. PROMONTORY | | W. Criticize sharply |
| V - 24. BRUTAL | | X. Lizard-like |
| A - 25. VIVACITY | | Y. Rebellious |

Odyssey Vocabulary  Matching 2

___ 1. CONTENDING
___ 2. SURMISED
___ 3. CLARION
___ 4. PATRIMONY
___ 5. REBUKE
___ 6. BALSAM
___ 7. COLLOQUY
___ 8. BRUTAL
___ 9. STEEPED
___10. ANODYNE
___11. WIELDING
___12. DISPERSED
___13. TAUT
___14. CHATTELS
___15. LOB
___16. PREVAILS
___17. FARCE
___18. BIER
___19. HOVERED
___20. AUGURY
___21. VAUNT
___22. SCORE
___23. MEAGER
___24. CODDLED
___25. PITH

A. Floated as if suspended
B. Inferred without conclusive evidence; guessed; gathered
C. Group of twenty items
D. Articles of personal, movable property; slaves
E. Striving in battle or controversy
F. Pulled or drawn tight
G. Hit, toss, or propel in a high arc
H. Triumphs or wins
I. Criticize sharply
J. Soaked
K. Interpreting signs and omens
L. Inheritance from a father
M. Tree that yields an aromatic, sticky substance
N. Cruel or harsh
O. Scattered in different directions
P. Handling a weapon or a tool
Q. Treated indulgently; babied
R. Formal conversation
S. Empty show; mockery
T. Shrill and clear
U. Boast or brag
V. Essential or central part of anything
W. Anything that soothes or confronts
X. Small in quantity, fullness, or extent
Y. Stand on which a coffin or corpse is placed

Odyssey Vocabulary  Matching 2 Answer Key

| | |
|---|---|
| E - 1. CONTENDING | A. Floated as if suspended |
| B - 2. SURMISED | B. Inferred without conclusive evidence; guessed; gathered |
| T - 3. CLARION | C. Group of twenty items |
| L - 4. PATRIMONY | D. Articles of personal, movable property; slaves |
| I - 5. REBUKE | E. Striving in battle or controversy |
| M - 6. BALSAM | F. Pulled or drawn tight |
| R - 7. COLLOQUY | G. Hit, toss, or propel in a high arc |
| N - 8. BRUTAL | H. Triumphs or wins |
| J - 9. STEEPED | I. Criticize sharply |
| W -10. ANODYNE | J. Soaked |
| P -11. WIELDING | K. Interpreting signs and omens |
| O -12. DISPERSED | L. Inheritance from a father |
| F -13. TAUT | M. Tree that yields an aromatic, sticky substance |
| D -14. CHATTELS | N. Cruel or harsh |
| G -15. LOB | O. Scattered in different directions |
| H -16. PREVAILS | P. Handling a weapon or a tool |
| S -17. FARCE | Q. Treated indulgently; babied |
| Y -18. BIER | R. Formal conversation |
| A -19. HOVERED | S. Empty show; mockery |
| K -20. AUGURY | T. Shrill and clear |
| U -21. VAUNT | U. Boast or brag |
| C -22. SCORE | V. Essential or central part of anything |
| X -23. MEAGER | W. Anything that soothes or confronts |
| Q -24. CODDLED | X. Small in quantity, fullness, or extent |
| V -25. PITH | Y. Stand on which a coffin or corpse is placed |

Odyssey Vocabulary Matching 3

___ 1. MEAGER
___ 2. WINDFALL
___ 3. DEFERENCE
___ 4. ADZE
___ 5. IMPLACABLE
___ 6. DERELICT
___ 7. BIER
___ 8. CONTENDING
___ 9. INTAGLIO
___ 10. FARCE
___ 11. MINIONS
___ 12. SAURIAN
___ 13. ANODYNE
___ 14. CLEFT
___ 15. RESPLENDENT
___ 16. DOLE
___ 17. SURMISED
___ 18. CALAMITOUS
___ 19. CACHE
___ 20. HALYARDS
___ 21. APPALLED
___ 22. PRECEDENCE
___ 23. DISTAFF
___ 24. VIE
___ 25. CLARION

A. Stick on a spinning wheel that holds unspun wool
B. Sudden and unexpected piece of good fortune
C. Vagrant or social outcast
D. Axe-like tool with arched blade at right angles to the handle
E. Design incised beneath the surface of metal
F. Striving in battle or controversy
G. Ropes used to raise or lower a sail or flag
H. Incapable of being pleased
I. Inferred without conclusive evidence; guessed; gathered
J. Division, separation
K. Small in quantity, fullness, or extent
L. To compete or strive for victory
M. Brilliant
N. Distribute in small portions
O. Filled with dismay
P. Anything that soothes or confronts
Q. Lizard-like
R. Empty show; mockery
S. Employees or domestic servants
T. Priority; going in advance
U. Stand on which a coffin or corpse is placed
V. Shrill and clear
W. Causing or involving a disaster
X. Courteous respect
Y. Hole or hiding place

Odyssey Vocabulary  Matching 3 Answer Key

| | |
|---|---|
| K - 1. MEAGER | A. Stick on a spinning wheel that holds unspun wool |
| B - 2. WINDFALL | B. Sudden and unexpected piece of good fortune |
| X - 3. DEFERENCE | C. Vagrant or social outcast |
| D - 4. ADZE | D. Axe-like tool with arched blade at right angles to the handle |
| H - 5. IMPLACABLE | E. Design incised beneath the surface of metal |
| C - 6. DERELICT | F. Striving in battle or controversy |
| U - 7. BIER | G. Ropes used to raise or lower a sail or flag |
| F - 8. CONTENDING | H. Incapable of being pleased |
| E - 9. INTAGLIO | I. Inferred without conclusive evidence; guessed; gathered |
| R -10. FARCE | J. Division, separation |
| S -11. MINIONS | K. Small in quantity, fullness, or extent |
| Q -12. SAURIAN | L. To compete or strive for victory |
| P -13. ANODYNE | M. Brilliant |
| J -14. CLEFT | N. Distribute in small portions |
| M -15. RESPLENDENT | O. Filled with dismay |
| N -16. DOLE | P. Anything that soothes or confronts |
| I - 17. SURMISED | Q. Lizard-like |
| W -18. CALAMITOUS | R. Empty show; mockery |
| Y -19. CACHE | S. Employees or domestic servants |
| G -20. HALYARDS | T. Priority; going in advance |
| O -21. APPALLED | U. Stand on which a coffin or corpse is placed |
| T -22. PRECEDENCE | V. Shrill and clear |
| A -23. DISTAFF | W. Causing or involving a disaster |
| L -24. VIE | X. Courteous respect |
| V -25. CLARION | Y. Hole or hiding place |

Copyrighted

Odyssey Vocabulary  Matching 4

___ 1. ARROGANCE         A. Water that collects in the low part of a ship's hull
___ 2. MUTINOUS          B. Employees or domestic servants
___ 3. SCORE             C. Sudden and unexpected piece of good fortune
___ 4. WINDFALL          D. Group of twenty items
___ 5. PITH              E. Brilliant
___ 6. PROWESS           F. Pulled or drawn tight
___ 7. DEFERENCE         G. Courteous respect
___ 8. BILGE             H. Emitting self-generated light
___ 9. STALWART          I. The act of destroying completely
___ 10. RESPLENDENT      J. Boast or brag
___ 11. VIGILANCE        K. Essential or central part of anything
___ 12. WANED            L. Rebellious
___ 13. PROFUSION        M. Inheritance from a father
___ 14. PRODIGIOUS       N. Watchfulness
___ 15. LOB              O. Lizard-like
___ 16. SAURIAN          P. Abundance; extravagance
___ 17. MINIONS          Q. Impressively great in size
___ 18. LIBATION         R. Insolent pride
___ 19. SUPPLICATION     S. Approached an end
___ 20. PATRIMONY        T. Superior skill or ability
___ 21. VAUNT            U. Liquid offering as a part of a religious ritual; intoxicating liquid
___ 22. RANCOR           V. Having physical strength
___ 23. ANNIHILATION     W. Plea; asking for humbly or earnestly
___ 24. TAUT             X. Hit, toss, or propel in a high arc
___ 25. LUMINOUS         Y. Bitter, long-lasting resentment

Odyssey Vocabulary  Matching 4 Answer Key

| | | |
|---|---|---|
| R - 1. ARROGANCE | A. | Water that collects in the low part of a ship's hull |
| L - 2. MUTINOUS | B. | Employees or domestic servants |
| D - 3. SCORE | C. | Sudden and unexpected piece of good fortune |
| C - 4. WINDFALL | D. | Group of twenty items |
| K - 5. PITH | E. | Brilliant |
| T - 6. PROWESS | F. | Pulled or drawn tight |
| G - 7. DEFERENCE | G. | Courteous respect |
| A - 8. BILGE | H. | Emitting self-generated light |
| V - 9. STALWART | I. | The act of destroying completely |
| E -10. RESPLENDENT | J. | Boast or brag |
| N -11. VIGILANCE | K. | Essential or central part of anything |
| S -12. WANED | L. | Rebellious |
| P -13. PROFUSION | M. | Inheritance from a father |
| Q -14. PRODIGIOUS | N. | Watchfulness |
| X -15. LOB | O. | Lizard-like |
| O -16. SAURIAN | P. | Abundance; extravagance |
| B -17. MINIONS | Q. | Impressively great in size |
| U -18. LIBATION | R. | Insolent pride |
| W -19. SUPPLICATION | S. | Approached an end |
| M -20. PATRIMONY | T. | Superior skill or ability |
| J - 21. VAUNT | U. | Liquid offering as a part of a religious ritual; intoxicating liquid |
| Y -22. RANCOR | V. | Having physical strength |
| I - 23. ANNIHILATION | W. | Plea; asking for humbly or earnestly |
| F - 24. TAUT | X. | Hit, toss, or propel in a high arc |
| H -25. LUMINOUS | Y. | Bitter, long-lasting resentment |

Odyssey Vocabulary  Magic Squares 1

Match the definition with the vocabulary word.  Put your answers in the magic squares below.  When your answers are correct, all columns and rows will add to the same number.

A. INTAGLIO
B. MUSTER
C. TYRO
D. AUDACITY
E. FETTLE
F. VIE
G. STINTED
H. BILGE
I. CORSAIRS
J. GUILE
K. PATRIMONY
L. REBUKE
M. WINDFALL
N. PERPLEXITY
O. FLOUT
P. PLUNDERED

1. Water that collects in the low part of a ship's hull
2. Sudden and unexpected piece of good fortune
3. Assemble or gather together
4. Inheritance from a father
5. Craftiness
6. Beginner or inexperienced person
7. Robbed of goods by force
8. Proper or sound condition; good spirits
9. Show contempt or scorn
10. To compete or strive for victory
11. Pirates
12. Boldness or daring
13. Design incised beneath the surface of metal
14. Criticize sharply
15. Restricted or limited
16. State of being puzzled or confused

| A= | B= | C= | D= |
| E= | F= | G= | H= |
| I= | J= | K= | L= |
| M= | N= | O= | P= |

Odyssey Vocabulary  Magic Squares 1 Answer Key

Match the definition with the vocabulary word.  Put your answers in the magic squares below.  When your answers are correct, all columns and rows will add to the same number.

A. INTAGLIO
B. MUSTER
C. TYRO
D. AUDACITY
E. FETTLE
F. VIE
G. STINTED
H. BILGE
I. CORSAIRS
J. GUILE
K. PATRIMONY
L. REBUKE
M. WINDFALL
N. PERPLEXITY
O. FLOUT
P. PLUNDERED

1. Water that collects in the low part of a ship's hull
2. Sudden and unexpected piece of good fortune
3. Assemble or gather together
4. Inheritance from a father
5. Craftiness
6. Beginner or inexperienced person
7. Robbed of goods by force
8. Proper or sound condition; good spirits
9. Show contempt or scorn
10. To compete or strive for victory
11. Pirates
12. Boldness or daring
13. Design incised beneath the surface of metal
14. Criticize sharply
15. Restricted or limited
16. State of being puzzled or confused

| A=13 | B=3  | C=6  | D=12 |
| ---- | ---- | ---- | ---- |
| E=8  | F=10 | G=15 | H=1  |
| I=11 | J=5  | K=4  | L=14 |
| M=2  | N=16 | O=9  | P=7  |

Odyssey Vocabulary  Magic Squares 2

Match the definition with the vocabulary word. Put your answers in the magic squares below. When your answers are correct, all columns and rows will add to the same number.

A. STEEPED
B. CODDLED
C. MUSTER
D. PLUNDERED
E. DEFERENCE
F. CALAMITOUS
G. SCORE
H. WINDFALL
I. SUPPLICATION
J. SURMISED
K. TAUT
L. FLOUT
M. DESOLATE
N. ADZE
O. TACTICIAN
P. CORSAIRS

1. Assemble or gather together
2. Inferred without conclusive evidence; guessed; gathered
3. Causing or involving a disaster
4. A person skilled in maneuvering
5. Pirates
6. Courteous respect
7. Plea; asking for humbly or earnestly
8. Robbed of goods by force
9. Deserted; dreary, gloomy
10. Sudden and unexpected piece of good fortune
11. Show contempt or scorn
12. Soaked
13. Treated indulgently; babied
14. Pulled or drawn tight
15. Group of twenty items
16. Axe-like tool with arched blade at right angles to the handle

| A= | B= | C= | D= |
|---|---|---|---|
| E= | F= | G= | H= |
| I= | J= | K= | L= |
| M= | N= | O= | P= |

Odyssey Vocabulary  Magic Squares 2 Answer Key

Match the definition with the vocabulary word.  Put your answers in the magic squares below.  When your answers are correct, all columns and rows will add to the same number.

A. STEEPED
B. CODDLED
C. MUSTER
D. PLUNDERED
E. DEFERENCE
F. CALAMITOUS
G. SCORE
H. WINDFALL
I. SUPPLICATION
J. SURMISED
K. TAUT
L. FLOUT
M. DESOLATE
N. ADZE
O. TACTICIAN
P. CORSAIRS

1. Assemble or gather together
2. Inferred without conclusive evidence; guessed; gathered
3. Causing or involving a disaster
4. A person skilled in maneuvering
5. Pirates
6. Courteous respect
7. Plea; asking for humbly or earnestly
8. Robbed of goods by force
9. Deserted; dreary, gloomy
10. Sudden and unexpected piece of good fortune
11. Show contempt or scorn
12. Soaked
13. Treated indulgently; babied
14. Pulled or drawn tight
15. Group of twenty items
16. Axe-like tool with arched blade at right angles to the handle

| A=12 | B=13 | C=1 | D=8 |
|---|---|---|---|
| E=6 | F=3 | G=15 | H=10 |
| I=7 | J=2 | K=14 | L=11 |
| M=9 | N=16 | O=4 | P=5 |

Odyssey Vocabulary Magic Squares 3

Match the definition with the vocabulary word. Put your answers in the magic squares below. When your answers are correct, all columns and rows will add to the same number.

A. DEFERENCE
B. PROMONTORY
C. CLEFT
D. VIVACITY
E. DOLE
F. RETAINER
G. CACHE
H. MINIONS
I. GUILE
J. TUMULT
K. CONTENTIOUSLY
L. AUGURY
M. PATRIMONY
N. PROFUSION
O. BRUTAL
P. OBLIVION

1. Employees or domestic servants
2. Courteous respect
3. High ridge of land or rock jutting into the sea
4. Hole or hiding place
5. Disorderly commotion
6. Cruel or harsh
7. State of being completely forgotten
8. Craftiness
9. In a quarrelsome way
10. Abundance; extravagance
11. Inheritance from a father
12. Interpreting signs and omens
13. Distribute in small portions
14. Liveliness
15. Division, separation
16. Subordinates of an organization or an individual

| A= | B= | C= | D= |
|---|---|---|---|
| E= | F= | G= | H= |
| I= | J= | K= | L= |
| M= | N= | O= | P= |

Odyssey Vocabulary Magic Squares 3 Answer Key

Match the definition with the vocabulary word. Put your answers in the magic squares below. When your answers are correct, all columns and rows will add to the same number.

A. DEFERENCE
B. PROMONTORY
C. CLEFT
D. VIVACITY
E. DOLE
F. RETAINER
G. CACHE
H. MINIONS
I. GUILE
J. TUMULT
K. CONTENTIOUSLY
L. AUGURY
M. PATRIMONY
N. PROFUSION
O. BRUTAL
P. OBLIVION

1. Employees or domestic servants
2. Courteous respect
3. High ridge of land or rock jutting into the sea
4. Hole or hiding place
5. Disorderly commotion
6. Cruel or harsh
7. State of being completely forgotten
8. Craftiness
9. In a quarrelsome way
10. Abundance; extravagance
11. Inheritance from a father
12. Interpreting signs and omens
13. Distribute in small portions
14. Liveliness
15. Division, separation
16. Subordinates of an organization or an individual

| A=2 | B=3 | C=15 | D=14 |
|---|---|---|---|
| E=13 | F=16 | G=4 | H=1 |
| I=8 | J=5 | K=9 | L=12 |
| M=11 | N=10 | O=6 | P=7 |

Odyssey Vocabulary  Magic Squares 4

Match the definition with the vocabulary word. Put your answers in the magic squares below. When your answers are correct, all columns and rows will add to the same number.

A. ARROGANCE
B. TUMULT
C. SAURIAN
D. GUILE
E. HARANGUED
F. PROWESS
G. MINIONS
H. FEIGN
I. BALSAM
J. PRECEDENCE
K. LUMINOUS
L. PROMONTORY
M. BIER
N. SUCCUMBED
O. SCORE
P. VALOR

1. Yielded or submitted to an overpowering force
2. Employees or domestic servants
3. High ridge of land or rock jutting into the sea
4. Insolent pride
5. Emitting self-generated light
6. Disorderly commotion
7. Stand on which a coffin or corpse is placed
8. Pretend
9. Delivered a long, strong-feeling speech
10. Courage and boldness
11. Lizard-like
12. Priority; going in advance
13. Craftiness
14. Tree that yields an aromatic, sticky substance
15. Superior skill or ability
16. Group of twenty items

| A= | B= | C= | D= |
|---|---|---|---|
| E= | F= | G= | H= |
| I= | J= | K= | L= |
| M= | N= | O= | P= |

Odyssey Vocabulary Magic Squares 4 Answer Key

Match the definition with the vocabulary word. Put your answers in the magic squares below. When your answers are correct, all columns and rows will add to the same number.

A. ARROGANCE
B. TUMULT
C. SAURIAN
D. GUILE
E. HARANGUED
F. PROWESS
G. MINIONS
H. FEIGN
I. BALSAM
J. PRECEDENCE
K. LUMINOUS
L. PROMONTORY
M. BIER
N. SUCCUMBED
O. SCORE
P. VALOR

1. Yielded or submitted to an overpowering force
2. Employees or domestic servants
3. High ridge of land or rock jutting into the sea
4. Insolent pride
5. Emitting self-generated light
6. Disorderly commotion
7. Stand on which a coffin or corpse is placed
8. Pretend
9. Delivered a long, strong-feeling speech
10. Courage and boldness
11. Lizard-like
12. Priority; going in advance
13. Craftiness
14. Tree that yields an aromatic, sticky substance
15. Superior skill or ability
16. Group of twenty items

| A=4 | B=6 | C=11 | D=13 |
| --- | --- | --- | --- |
| E=9 | F=15 | G=2 | H=8 |
| I=14 | J=12 | K=5 | L=3 |
| M=7 | N=1 | O=16 | P=10 |

## Odyssey Vocabulary Word Search 1

Words are placed backwards, forward, diagonally, up and down. Clues listed below can help you find the words. Circle the hidden vocabulary words in the maze.

```
L I B A T I O N R C L A R I O N C Y
C O L G N I D N E T N O C Z L R O D
N H B W U W N W B O B L I V I O N R
J O A V A F A D U F X A X B V M T Q
Z V L F V K J N K N M T S L I B E R
S E S J F N G I E F G U I L E L N Q
U R A B Q T V C B D O R S N M O T K
R E M W R U R V J T M B E T I R I J
M D I S T A F F I D R V A T E N O J
I C J C F T C M B O O D A T A R U B
S O C O F S A E L Z C B I W P S G
E L T R H L L A E E I O C I D E L T
D L U E A K V N G L R I A C E T Y P
X O M C P N T L P Y T S C A T R R B
K Q U N L C I P T C N L H N N E U M
T U L C E B U N A B E T E D I L G N
Z Y T R S S P T G F I W Y O T S U X
S R I A S R O C T P L C T R S Q A L
```

A pair (5)
A person skilled in maneuvering (9)
Approached an end (5)
Assemble or gather together (6)
Axe-like tool with arched blade at right angles to the handle (4)
Beginner or inexperienced person (4)
Boast or brag (5)
Causing or involving a disaster (10)
Courage and boldness (5)
Craftiness (5)
Criticize sharply (6)
Cruel or harsh (6)
Disorderly commotion (6)
Distribute in small portions (4)
Division, separation (5)
Empty show; mockery (5)
Essential or central part of anything (4)
Floated as if suspended (7)
Formal conversation (8)
Frankness; sincerity (6)
Group of twenty items (5)
Hit, toss, or propel in a high arc (3)
Hole or hiding place (5)
In a quarrelsome way (13)
Inferred without conclusive evidence; guessed; gathered (8)
Interpreting signs and omens (6)
Kind (10)
Liquid offering as a part of a religious ritual; intoxicating liquid (8)
Luckless; unfortunate (7)
Pirates (8)
Plea; asking for humbly or earnestly (12)
Pretend (5)
Pulled or drawn tight (4)
Restricted or limited (7)
Sea birds (7)
Shrill and clear (7)
Stand on which a coffin or corpse is placed (4)
State of being completely forgotten (8)
Stick on a spinning wheel that holds unspun wool (7)
Stretching and straining (7)
Striving in battle or controversy (10)
To compete or strive for victory (3)
Tree that yields an aromatic, sticky substance (6)
Water that collects in the low part of a ship's hull (5)

# Odyssey Vocabulary Word Search 1 Answer Key

Words are placed backwards, forward, diagonally, up and down. Clues listed below can help you find the words. Circle the hidden vocabulary words in the maze.

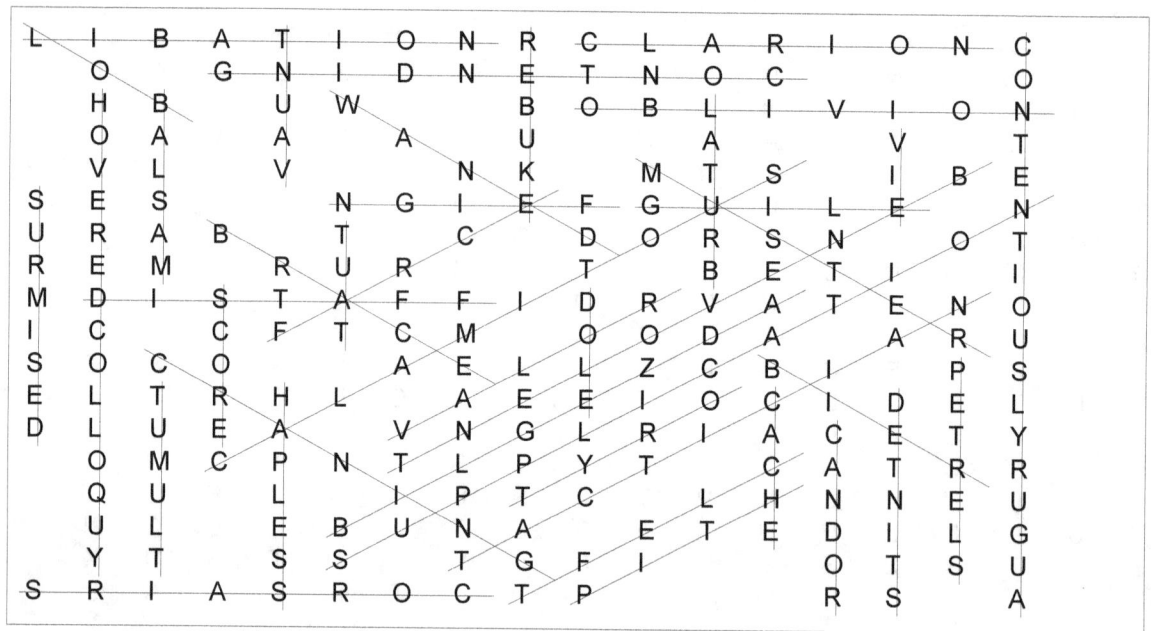

A pair (5)
A person skilled in maneuvering (9)
Approached an end (5)
Assemble or gather together (6)
Axe-like tool with arched blade at right angles to the handle (4)
Beginner or inexperienced person (4)
Boast or brag (5)
Causing or involving a disaster (10)
Courage and boldness (5)
Craftiness (5)
Criticize sharply (6)
Cruel or harsh (6)
Disorderly commotion (6)
Distribute in small portions (4)
Division, separation (5)
Empty show; mockery (5)
Essential or central part of anything (4)
Floated as if suspended (7)
Formal conversation (8)
Frankness; sincerity (6)
Group of twenty items (5)
Hit, toss, or propel in a high arc (3)
Hole or hiding place (5)
In a quarrelsome way (13)
Inferred without conclusive evidence; guessed; gathered (8)
Interpreting signs and omens (6)
Kind (10)
Liquid offering as a part of a religious ritual; intoxicating liquid (8)
Luckless; unfortunate (7)
Pirates (8)
Plea; asking for humbly or earnestly (12)
Pretend (5)
Pulled or drawn tight (4)
Restricted or limited (7)
Sea birds (7)
Shrill and clear (7)
Stand on which a coffin or corpse is placed (4)
State of being completely forgotten (8)
Stick on a spinning wheel that holds unspun wool (7)
Stretching and straining (7)
Striving in battle or controversy (10)
To compete or strive for victory (3)
Tree that yields an aromatic, sticky substance (6)
Water that collects in the low part of a ship's hull (5)

Odyssey Vocabulary Word Search 2

Words are placed backwards, forward, diagonally, up and down. Clues listed below can help you find the words. Circle the hidden vocabulary words in the maze.

```
B R U T A L I M P L A C A B L E C N
B I K M N N B W F N O A A S D Z L K
H W L T G Z A M O M S N R C C D A H
Y Y Z G I N N D E G C D P M H A R T
S D O L E R Y L M T O O V E A E I F
C U G D F N Y H U R R R A A T S O H
Z O R Y E Z Y O P A E V U G T N W
X F L M G F L V L N P J N E E O V R
D E C O I F E E S C B U T R L I E Y
I T A L N S R R L O Z B N F S N S H
S T U S E N E E E R M R Z G I I T J
P L D U M F A D R N L A T A E M I T
E E A O X Q T D T R C C T Y Y N N B
R C C R E B U K E S S E W O R P T S
S R I O P N T T P H R G Q E U O E N
E A T M E U S Q T L E L I U G S D N
D F Y I A U P I C O J B T L U M U T
Z F V T M R P G O B S T I N A C Y X
```

A pair (5)
A sharp, bitter taste (7)
Anything that soothes or confronts (7)
Apprehensive; fearfully cautious (8)
Approached an end (5)
Articles of personal, movable property; slaves (8)
Assemble or gather together (6)
Attractive; handsome; graceful (6)
Axe-like tool with arched blade at right angles to the handle (4)
Beginner or inexperienced person (4)
Bitter, long-lasting resentment (6)
Boast or brag (5)
Boldness or daring (8)
Courteous respect (9)
Craftiness (5)
Criticize sharply (6)
Cruel or harsh (6)
Disorderly commotion (6)
Distribute in small portions (4)
Division, separation (5)
Employees or domestic servants (7)
Empty show; mockery (5)
Essential or central part of anything (4)
Floated as if suspended (7)

Frankness; sincerity (6)
Group of twenty items (5)
Hit, toss, or propel in a high arc (3)
Hole or hiding place (5)
Incapable of being pleased (10)
Inferred without conclusive evidence; guessed; gathered (8)
Interpreting signs and omens (6)
Pretend (5)
Proper or sound condition; good spirits (6)
Pulled or drawn tight (4)
Restricted or limited (7)
Scattered in different directions (9)
Sea birds (7)
Series of columns placed at regular intervals (9)
Show contempt or scorn (5)
Shrill and clear (7)
Small in quantity, fullness, or extent (6)
Stand on which a coffin or corpse is placed (4)
Stubbornness (9)
Subordinates of an organization or an individual (8)
Superior skill or ability (7)
To compete or strive for victory (3)
Water that collects in the low part of a ship's hull (5)

Odyssey Vocabulary Word Search 2 Answer Key

Words are placed backwards, forward, diagonally, up and down. Clues listed below can help you find the words. Circle the hidden vocabulary words in the maze.

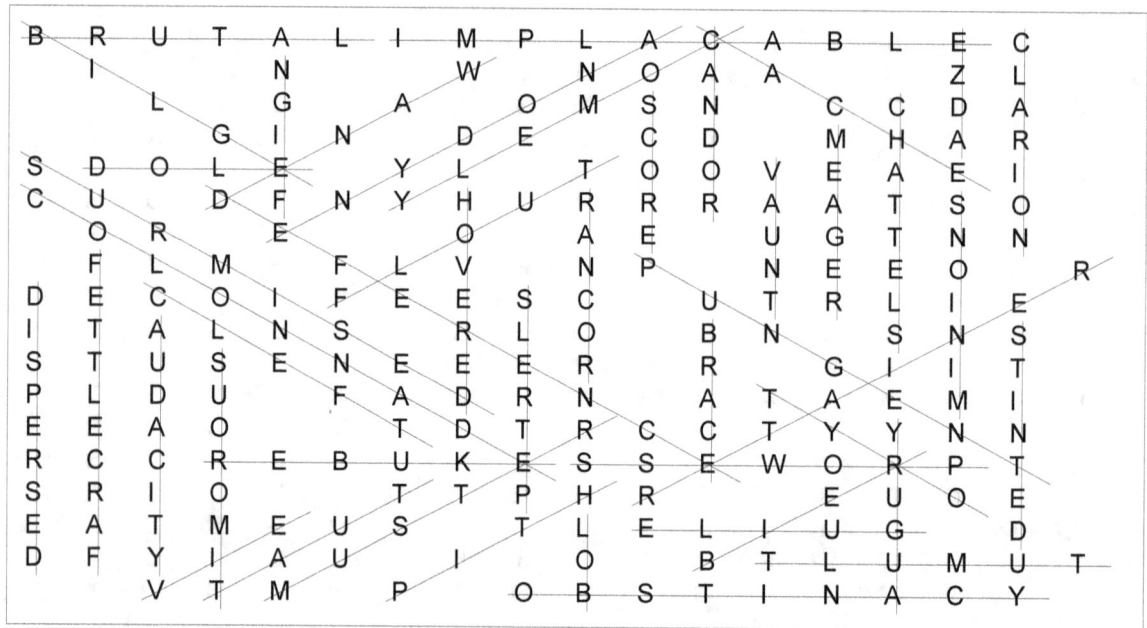

A pair (5)
A sharp, bitter taste (7)
Anything that soothes or confronts (7)
Apprehensive; fearfully cautious (8)
Approached an end (5)
Articles of personal, movable property; slaves (8)
Assemble or gather together (6)
Attractive; handsome; graceful (6)
Axe-like tool with arched blade at right angles to the handle (4)
Beginner or inexperienced person (4)
Bitter, long-lasting resentment (6)
Boast or brag (5)
Boldness or daring (8)
Courteous respect (9)
Craftiness (5)
Criticize sharply (6)
Cruel or harsh (6)
Disorderly commotion (6)
Distribute in small portions (4)
Division, separation (5)
Employees or domestic servants (7)
Empty show; mockery (5)
Essential or central part of anything (4)
Floated as if suspended (7)

Frankness; sincerity (6)
Group of twenty items (5)
Hit, toss, or propel in a high arc (3)
Hole or hiding place (5)
Incapable of being pleased (10)
Inferred without conclusive evidence; guessed; gathered (8)
Interpreting signs and omens (6)
Pretend (5)
Proper or sound condition; good spirits (6)
Pulled or drawn tight (4)
Restricted or limited (7)
Scattered in different directions (9)
Sea birds (7)
Series of columns placed at regular intervals (9)
Show contempt or scorn (5)
Shrill and clear (7)
Small in quantity, fullness, or extent (6)
Stand on which a coffin or corpse is placed (4)
Stubbornness (9)
Subordinates of an organization or an individual (8)
Superior skill or ability (7)
To compete or strive for victory (3)
Water that collects in the low part of a ship's hull (5)

Odyssey Vocabulary  Word Search 3

Words are placed backwards, forward, diagonally, up and down. Words listed below are included in the maze. Circle the hidden vocabulary words in the maze.

```
B A L S A M O R D A I N E D T R R B
R T S U M Y V F Y B V M E H E E F L
E F X O E H A P L E S S L N T P L M
B C M T A Z L F E I G N I S H R O R
U P Z I G V O L M F Q A U C A O U F
K H M M E D R A O I T M G R U W T V
E Y O A R P Y T C E N Q H Z G E T Q
P T R L O W U U R N C I L W U S Y N
U I T A C R Q R V O J D O A R S Y E
N C I C S O O B L I V I O N Y K L R
G A F T D D L J R T P B A E S T A P
E V I U C N L U G A T I I D T N L D
N I E A H A O S M B C M D E C O O J
T V D T T C C N O I S U F O R P B V
S Z I N P L G H T L N H R Y L R I D
E P U E E L N C E C W O T B A E L S
M A C F L L A F D N I W U C V M G L
V S T I N T E D F A R C E S Z X E B
```

| ADZE | COMELY | MINIONS | SCORE |
|---|---|---|---|
| AUGURY | DOLE | MORTIFIED | STINTED |
| BALSAM | FARCE | MUSTER | TACTICIAN |
| BIER | FEIGN | OBLIVION | TAUT |
| BILGE | FETTLE | ORDAINED | TYRO |
| BRACE | FLOUT | PITH | VALOR |
| BRUTAL | GUILE | PROFUSION | VAUNT |
| CACHE | HAPLESS | PROWESS | VIE |
| CALAMITOUS | LIBATION | PUNGENT | VIVACITY |
| CANDOR | LOB | RANCOR | WANED |
| CLEFT | LUMINOUS | REBUKE | WINDFALL |
| COLLOQUY | MEAGER | RETAINER | |

Odyssey Vocabulary  Word Search 3 Answer Key

Words are placed backwards, forward, diagonally, up and down. Words listed below are included in the maze. Circle the hidden vocabulary words in the maze.

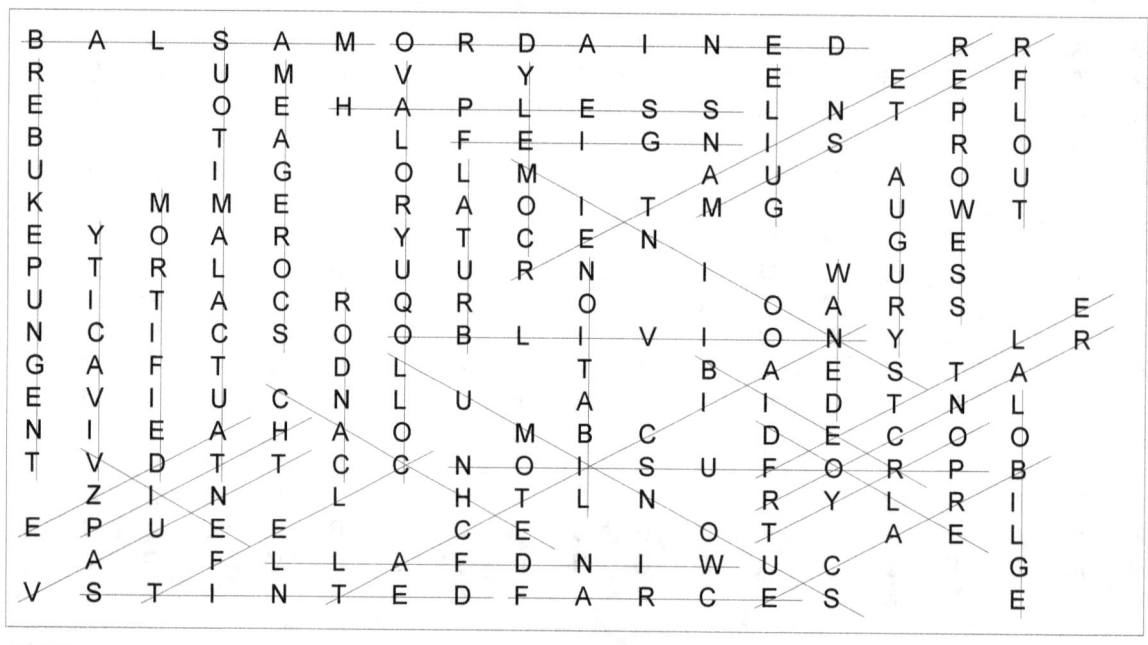

| ADZE | COMELY | MINIONS | SCORE |
| AUGURY | DOLE | MORTIFIED | STINTED |
| BALSAM | FARCE | MUSTER | TACTICIAN |
| BIER | FEIGN | OBLIVION | TAUT |
| BILGE | FETTLE | ORDAINED | TYRO |
| BRACE | FLOUT | PITH | VALOR |
| BRUTAL | GUILE | PROFUSION | VAUNT |
| CACHE | HAPLESS | PROWESS | VIE |
| CALAMITOUS | LIBATION | PUNGENT | VIVACITY |
| CANDOR | LOB | RANCOR | WANED |
| CLEFT | LUMINOUS | REBUKE | WINDFALL |
| COLLOQUY | MEAGER | RETAINER | |

Odyssey Vocabulary  Word Search 4

Words are placed backwards, forward, diagonally, up and down. Words listed below are included in the maze. Circle the hidden vocabulary words in the maze.

```
G K P V C A N D O R L P D A D Z E C
M U T I N O U S F A R C E O R Y T R
O D O G T N U A V E O G U T W F U J
R W B I W H B R T M L M G C R D M J
T C S L C P F S E I H E N A C E U Q
I O T A S S U L B Y D A A C L S L X
F R I N U M Y T O R I G R H E R T V
I S N C R R W W R U S E E Z F E S F
E A A E M V I E O G T R H Z T P T B
D I C R I W N A C U A M Y N C S E R
A R Y O S A D V N A F C E O E I E R
N S Y C E N F Q A S F L L Q C D P Y
N B T S D E A V R E O L I A A T E N
O R V I P D L H T V O B U S R M D S
L U D H N M L T E Q L O G B B I G F
O T A U T M L N U B A L S A M I O N
C A B X N E E Y O R D A I N E D P L
F L R E I B R D V A L O R F D O L E
```

| ADZE | COLONNADE | MEAGER | SURMISED |
| AUGURY | COMELY | MORTIFIED | TAUT |
| BALSAM | CORSAIRS | MUSTER | TUMULT |
| BENEVOLENT | DISPERSED | MUTINOUS | TYRO |
| BIER | DISTAFF | OBSTINACY | VALOR |
| BILGE | DOLE | ORDAINED | VAUNT |
| BRACE | FARCE | PETRELS | VIE |
| BRUTAL | FEIGN | PITH | VIGILANCE |
| CACHE | FETTLE | RANCOR | WANED |
| CANDOR | FLOUT | SAURIAN | WINDFALL |
| CLARION | GUILE | SCORE | |
| CLEFT | HARANGUED | STEEPED | |
| COLLOQUY | LOB | STINTED | |

# Odyssey Vocabulary Word Search 4 Answer Key

Words are placed backwards, forward, diagonally, up and down. Words listed below are included in the maze. Circle the hidden vocabulary words in the maze.

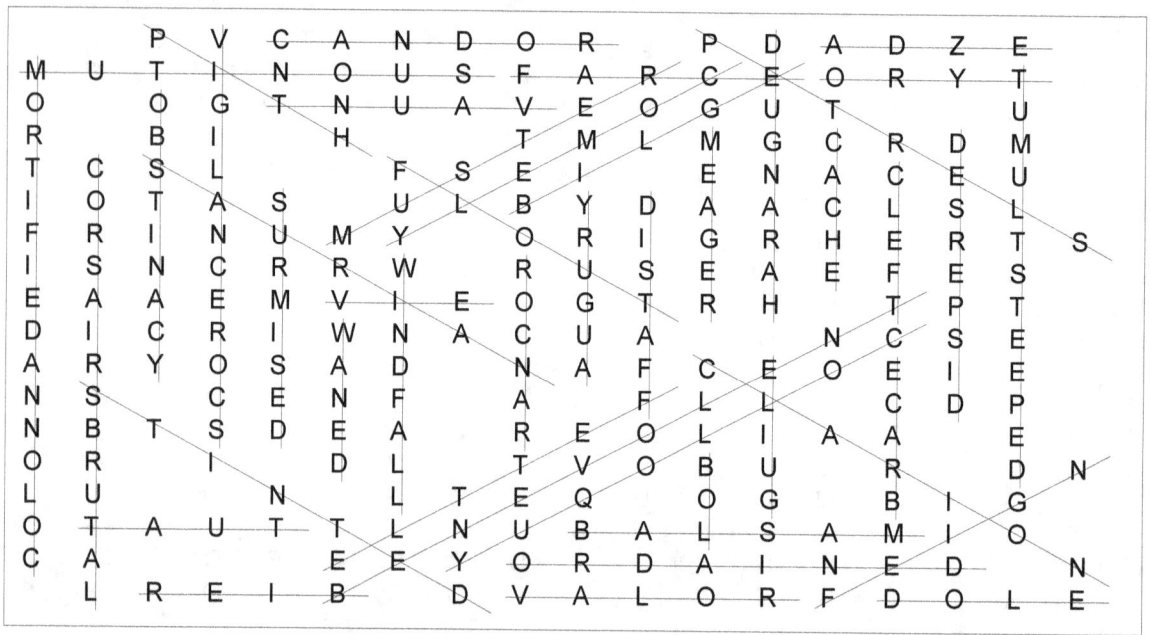

| ADZE | COLONNADE | MEAGER | SURMISED |
| AUGURY | COMELY | MORTIFIED | TAUT |
| BALSAM | CORSAIRS | MUSTER | TUMULT |
| BENEVOLENT | DISPERSED | MUTINOUS | TYRO |
| BIER | DISTAFF | OBSTINACY | VALOR |
| BILGE | DOLE | ORDAINED | VAUNT |
| BRACE | FARCE | PETRELS | VIE |
| BRUTAL | FEIGN | PITH | VIGILANCE |
| CACHE | FETTLE | RANCOR | WANED |
| CANDOR | FLOUT | SAURIAN | WINDFALL |
| CLARION | GUILE | SCORE | |
| CLEFT | HARANGUED | STEEPED | |
| COLLOQUY | LOB | STINTED | |

Odyssey Vocabulary Crossword 1

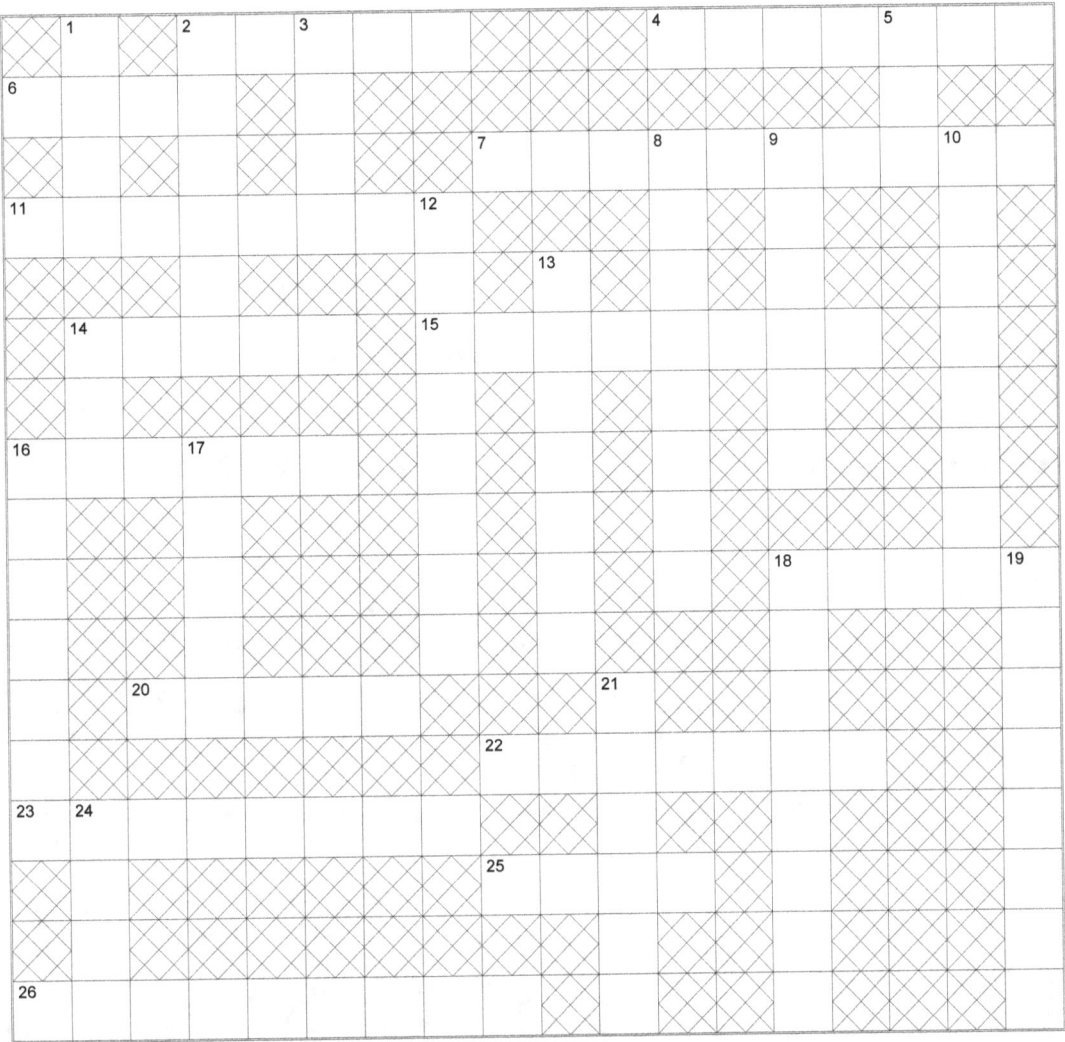

**Across**
2. A pair
4. Treated indulgently; babied
6. Stand on which a coffin or corpse is placed
7. Incapable of being pleased
11. Articles of personal, movable property; slaves
14. Courage and boldness
15. Subordinates of an organization or an individual
16. Small in quantity, fullness, or extent
18. Boast or brag
20. Pretend
22. Lizard-like
23. Having physical strength
25. Pulled or drawn tight
26. Series of columns placed at regular intervals

**Down**
1. Essential or central part of anything
2. Cruel or harsh
3. Axe-like tool with arched blade at right angles to the handle
5. Hit, toss, or propel in a high arc
8. Emitting self-generated light
9. Attractive; handsome; graceful
10. Liquid offering as a part of a religious ritual; intoxicating liquid
12. Inferred without conclusive evidence; guessed; gathered
13. Soaked
14. To compete or strive for victory
16. Employees or domestic servants
17. Craftiness
18. Liveliness
19. Apprehensive; fearfully cautious
21. Interpreting signs and omens
24. Beginner or inexperienced person

Odyssey Vocabulary  Crossword 1 Answer Key

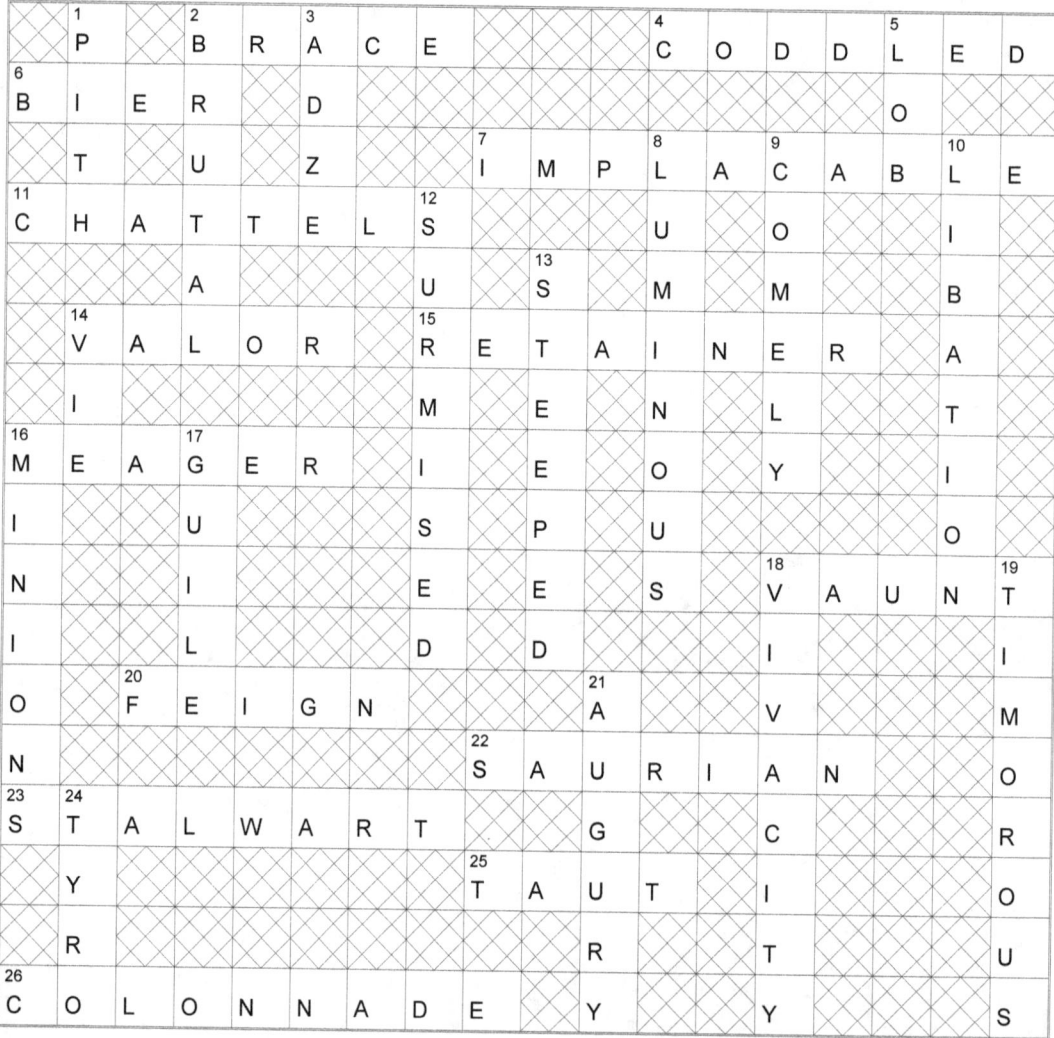

Across
2. A pair
4. Treated indulgently; babied
6. Stand on which a coffin or corpse is placed
7. Incapable of being pleased
11. Articles of personal, movable property; slaves
14. Courage and boldness
15. Subordinates of an organization or an individual
16. Small in quantity, fullness, or extent
18. Boast or brag
20. Pretend
22. Lizard-like
23. Having physical strength
25. Pulled or drawn tight
26. Series of columns placed at regular intervals

Down
1. Essential or central part of anything
2. Cruel or harsh
3. Axe-like tool with arched blade at right angles to the handle
5. Hit, toss, or propel in a high arc
8. Emitting self-generated light
9. Attractive; handsome; graceful
10. Liquid offering as a part of a religious ritual; intoxicating liquid
12. Inferred without conclusive evidence; guessed; gathered
13. Soaked
14. To compete or strive for victory
16. Employees or domestic servants
17. Craftiness
18. Liveliness
19. Apprehensive; fearfully cautious
21. Interpreting signs and omens
24. Beginner or inexperienced person

Odyssey Vocabulary Crossword 2

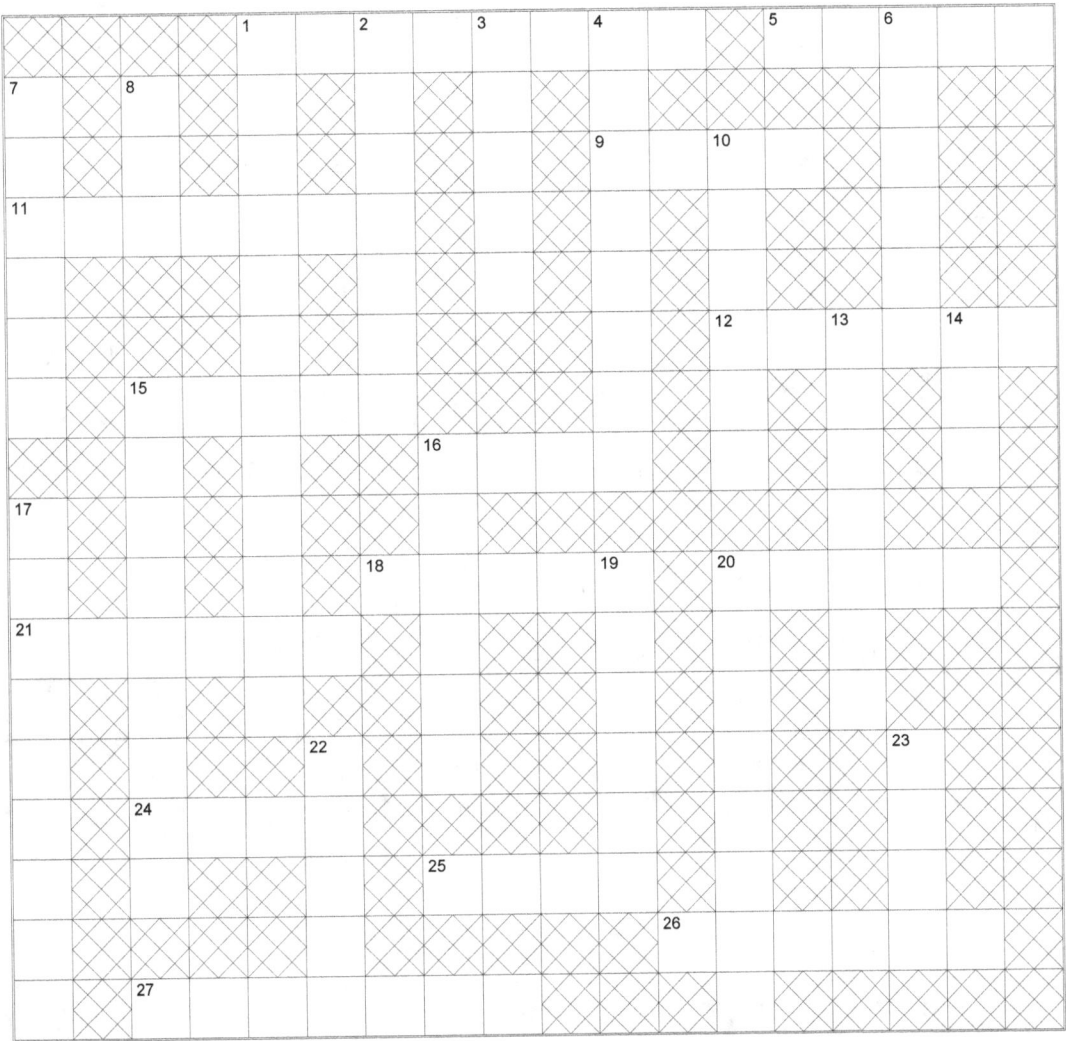

Across
1. Having physical strength
5. Empty show; mockery
9. Beginner or inexperienced person
11. Soaked
12. Attractive; handsome; graceful
15. Hole or hiding place
16. Stand on which a coffin or corpse is placed
18. Show contempt or scorn
20. Group of twenty items
21. Frankness; sincerity
24. Distribute in small portions
25. Pulled or drawn tight
26. Small in quantity, fullness, or extent
27. Stretching and straining

Down
1. Plea; asking for humbly or earnestly
2. Anything that soothes or confronts
3. Approached an end
4. Subordinates of an organization or an individual
6. Criticize sharply
7. Assemble or gather together
8. To compete or strive for victory
10. Bitter, long-lasting resentment
13. Employees or domestic servants
14. Hit, toss, or propel in a high arc
15. Series of columns placed at regular intervals
16. Tree that yields an aromatic, sticky substance
17. Yielded or submitted to an overpowering force
19. Disorderly commotion
20. Inferred without conclusive evidence; guessed; gathered
22. Pretend
23. Axe-like tool with arched blade at right angles to the handle

Odyssey Vocabulary  Crossword 2 Answer Key

|   |   |   | 1 S | 2 T | A | 3 L | W | A | 4 R | T |   | 5 F | 6 A | R | C | E |
|---|---|---|---|---|---|---|---|---|---|---|---|---|---|---|---|---|
| 7 M | | 8 V | | U | | N | | A | E | | | | E | | | |
| U | | I | | P | | O | | N | 9 T | Y | 10 R | O | B | | | |
| 11 S | T | E | E | P | E | D | | | A | | A | | U | | | |
| T | | | | L | | Y | | D | I | | N | | K | | | |
| E | | | | I | | N | | | N | | 12 C | O | 13 M | E | 14 L | Y |
| R | | 15 C | A | C | H | E | | | E | | O | | I | | O | |
| | | O | | A | | | 16 B | I | E | R | | | N | | B | |
| 17 S | | L | | T | | | A | | | | | | I | | | |
| U | | O | | I | | 18 F | L | O | 19 U | T | 20 S | C | O | R | E | |
| 21 C | A | N | D | O | R | S | | | U | | C | U | N | | | |
| C | | N | | N | | A | | | M | | R | S | | | | |
| U | | A | | | | 22 F | A | M | U | | M | | 23 A | | | |
| M | | 24 D | O | L | E | | | | L | | I | | D | | | |
| B | | E | | | | 25 T | A | U | T | | S | | Z | | | |
| E | | | | | | | | | 26 M | E | A | G | E | R | | |
| D | | 27 C | R | A | N | I | N | G | | | | | D | | | |

Across
1. Having physical strength
5. Empty show; mockery
9. Beginner or inexperienced person
11. Soaked
12. Attractive; handsome; graceful
15. Hole or hiding place
16. Stand on which a coffin or corpse is placed
18. Show contempt or scorn
20. Group of twenty items
21. Frankness; sincerity
24. Distribute in small portions
25. Pulled or drawn tight
26. Small in quantity, fullness, or extent
27. Stretching and straining

Down
1. Plea; asking for humbly or earnestly
2. Anything that soothes or confronts

3. Approached an end
4. Subordinates of an organization or an individual
6. Criticize sharply
7. Assemble or gather together
8. To compete or strive for victory
10. Bitter, long-lasting resentment
13. Employees or domestic servants
14. Hit, toss, or propel in a high arc
15. Series of columns placed at regular intervals
16. Tree that yields an aromatic, sticky substance
17. Yielded or submitted to an overpowering force
19. Disorderly commotion
20. Inferred without conclusive evidence; guessed; gathered
22. Pretend
23. Axe-like tool with arched blade at right angles to the handle

Odyssey Vocabulary Crossword 3

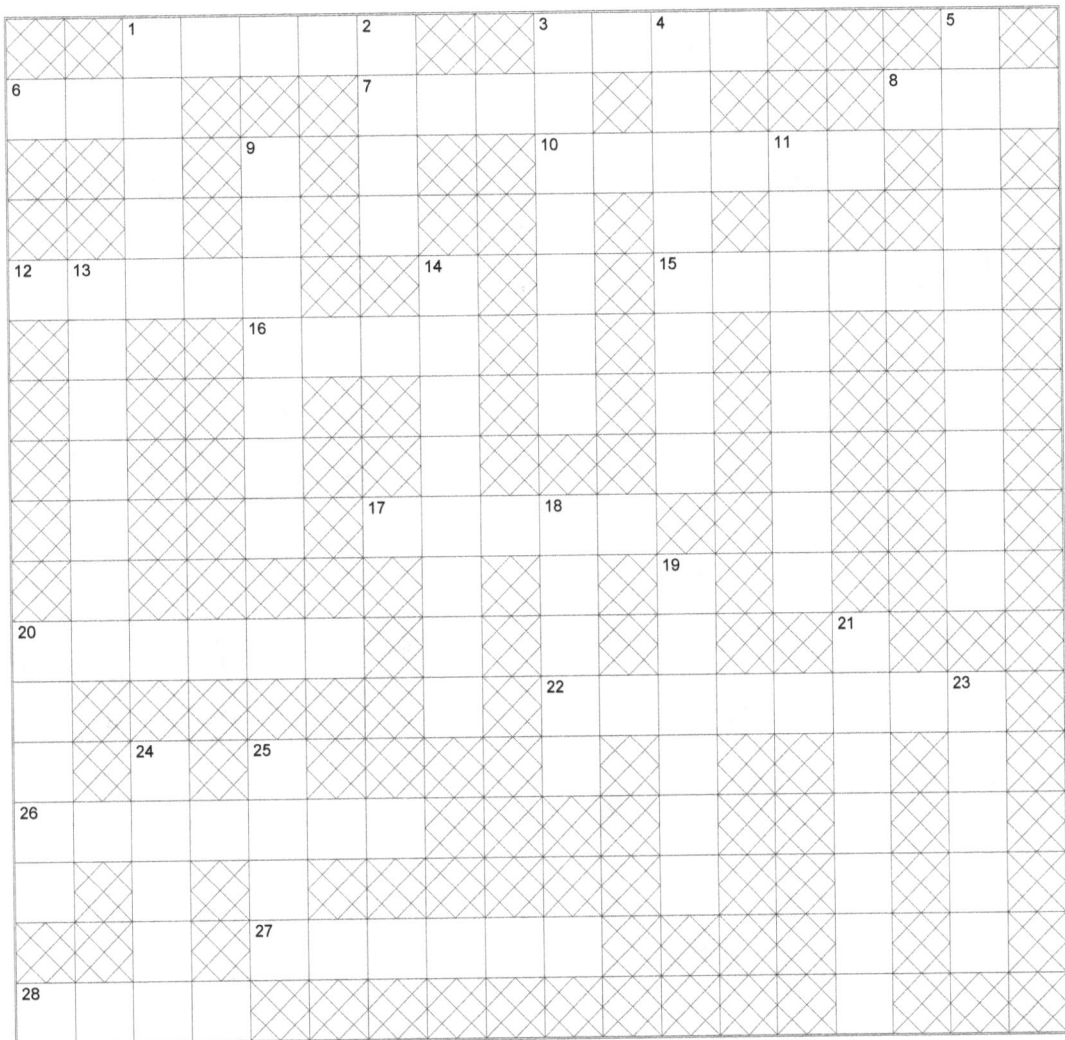

Across
1. Show contempt or scorn
3. Essential or central part of anything
6. To compete or strive for victory
7. Axe-like tool with arched blade at right angles to the handle
8. Hit, toss, or propel in a high arc
10. Disorderly commotion
12. Approached an end
15. Criticize sharply
16. Distribute in small portions
17. Water that collects in the low part of a ship's hull
20. Proper or sound condition; good spirits
22. Emitting self-generated light
26. Stretching and straining
27. Bitter, long-lasting resentment
28. Beginner or inexperienced person

Down
1. Pretend
2. Pulled or drawn tight
3. Sea birds
4. Apprehensive; fearfully cautious
5. Striving in battle or controversy
9. Treated indulgently; babied
11. Liquid offering as a part of a religious ritual; intoxicating liquid
13. Anything that soothes or confronts
14. Subordinates of an organization or an individual
18. Craftiness
19. Attractive; handsome; graceful
20. Empty show; mockery
21. Floated as if suspended
23. Group of twenty items
24. Courage and boldness
25. Stand on which a coffin or corpse is placed

Odyssey Vocabulary  Crossword 3 Answer Key

**Across**
1. Show contempt or scorn
3. Essential or central part of anything
6. To compete or strive for victory
7. Axe-like tool with arched blade at right angles to the handle
8. Hit, toss, or propel in a high arc
10. Disorderly commotion
12. Approached an end
15. Criticize sharply
16. Distribute in small portions
17. Water that collects in the low part of a ship's hull
20. Proper or sound condition; good spirits
22. Emitting self-generated light
26. Stretching and straining
27. Bitter, long-lasting resentment
28. Beginner or inexperienced person

**Down**
1. Pretend
2. Pulled or drawn tight
3. Sea birds
4. Apprehensive; fearfully cautious
5. Striving in battle or controversy
9. Treated indulgently; babied
11. Liquid offering as a part of a religious ritual; intoxicating liquid
13. Anything that soothes or confronts
14. Subordinates of an organization or an individual
18. Craftiness
19. Attractive; handsome; graceful
20. Empty show; mockery
21. Floated as if suspended
23. Group of twenty items
24. Courage and boldness
25. Stand on which a coffin or corpse is placed

Odyssey Vocabulary Crossword 4

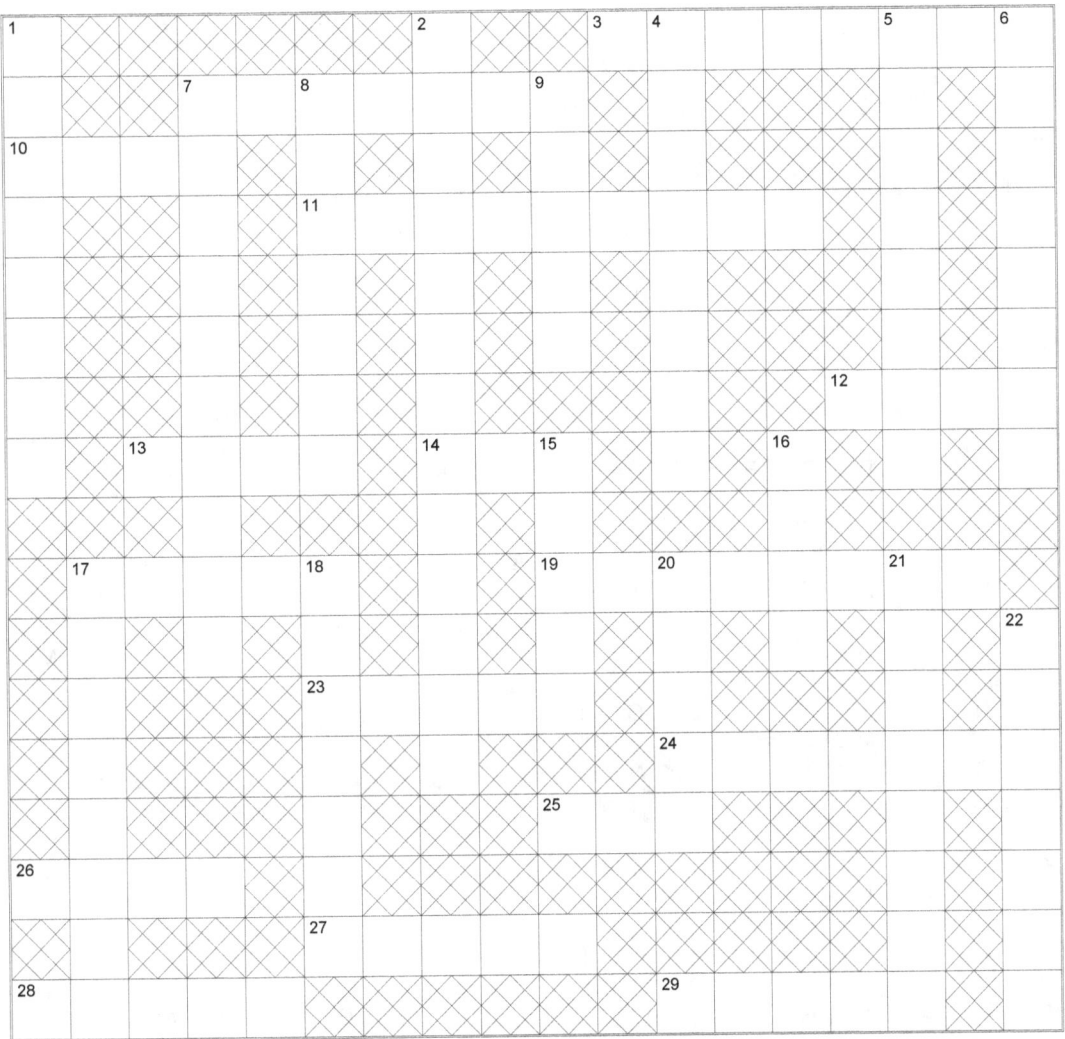

Across
- 3. Pirates
- 7. Stretching and straining
- 10. Beginner or inexperienced person
- 11. Stubbornness
- 12. Stand on which a coffin or corpse is placed
- 13. Axe-like tool with arched blade at right angles to the handle
- 14. Hit, toss, or propel in a high arc
- 17. Approached an end
- 19. Liquid offering as a part of a religious ritual; intoxicating liquid
- 23. Group of twenty items
- 24. Shrill and clear
- 25. To compete or strive for victory
- 26. Pulled or drawn tight
- 27. Empty show; mockery
- 28. Division, separation
- 29. Pretend

Down
- 1. Rebellious
- 2. Concealing or disguising
- 4. Prearranged; predestined
- 5. Design incised beneath the surface of metal
- 6. Having physical strength
- 7. Striving in battle or controversy
- 8. Anything that soothes or confronts
- 9. Craftiness
- 15. Water that collects in the low part of a ship's hull
- 16. Essential or central part of anything
- 17. Sudden and unexpected piece of good fortune
- 18. Stick on a spinning wheel that holds unspun wool
- 20. A pair
- 21. State of being completely forgotten
- 22. Employees or domestic servants

# Odyssey Vocabulary Crossword 4 Answer Key

|   |   |   |   |   |   |   |   |   |   |   |   |   |
|---|---|---|---|---|---|---|---|---|---|---|---|---|
| ¹M |   |   |   |   | ²D |   | ³C | ⁴O | R | S | ⁵A | I | R | ⁶S |
| U |   | ⁷C | ⁸R | A | N | I | N | ⁹G |   | R |   |   | N |   | T |
| ¹⁰T | Y | R | O |   | N | S |   | U |   | D |   |   | T |   | A |
| I |   | N |   | ¹¹O | B | S | T | I | N | A | C | Y |   | A |   | L |
| N |   | T |   | D |   | I |   | L |   | I |   |   |   | G |   | W |
| O |   | E |   | Y |   | M |   | E |   | N |   |   |   | L |   | A |
| U |   | N |   | N |   | U |   |   |   | E |   | ¹²B | I | E | R |
| ¹³S |   | A | D | Z | E | ¹⁴L | O | ¹⁵B |   | D |   | ¹⁶P | O |   | T |
|   |   | I |   |   |   | A |   | I |   |   |   | I |   |   |   |   |
|   | ¹⁷W | A | N | ¹⁸E | D |   | ¹⁹L | I | ²⁰B | A | T | I | ²¹O | N |   |
|   | I |   | G |   | I |   | I |   | G |   | R |   | H |   | B |   | ²²M |
|   | N |   |   | ²³S | C | O | R | E |   | A |   |   |   | L |   | I |
|   | D |   |   |   | T |   | N |   |   | ²⁴C | L | A | R | I | O | N |
|   | F |   |   |   | A |   |   | ²⁵V | I | E |   |   |   | V |   | I |
| ²⁶T | A | U | T |   | F |   |   |   |   |   |   |   |   | I |   | O |
|   | L |   |   |   | ²⁷F | A | R | C | E |   |   |   |   | O |   | N |
| ²⁸C | L | E | F | T |   |   |   |   |   | ²⁹F | E | I | G | N |   | S |

**Across**
3. Pirates
7. Stretching and straining
10. Beginner or inexperienced person
11. Stubbornness
12. Stand on which a coffin or corpse is placed
13. Axe-like tool with arched blade at right angles to the handle
14. Hit, toss, or propel in a high arc
17. Approached an end
19. Liquid offering as a part of a religious ritual; intoxicating liquid
23. Group of twenty items
24. Shrill and clear
25. To compete or strive for victory
26. Pulled or drawn tight
27. Empty show; mockery
28. Division, separation
29. Pretend

**Down**
1. Rebellious
2. Concealing or disguising
4. Prearranged; predestined
5. Design incised beneath the surface of metal
6. Having physical strength
7. Striving in battle or controversy
8. Anything that soothes or confronts
9. Craftiness
15. Water that collects in the low part of a ship's hull
16. Essential or central part of anything
17. Sudden and unexpected piece of good fortune
18. Stick on a spinning wheel that holds unspun wool
20. A pair
21. State of being completely forgotten
22. Employees or domestic servants

Odyssey Vocabulary  Juggle Letters 1

1. RELEITPYXP = 1. _____
State of being puzzled or confused

2. RUAGHDENA = 2. _____
Delivered a long, strong-feeling speech

3. REENPLDDU = 3. _____
Robbed of goods by force

4. IOCNALR = 4. _____
Shrill and clear

5. TNVEEENBOL = 5. _____
Kind

6. CRFAE = 6. _____
Empty show; mockery

7. SERIUDMS = 7. _____
Inferred without conclusive evidence; guessed; gathered

8. TCRIEELD = 8. _____
Vagrant or social outcast

9. OISINTSLIMAUD = 9. _____
Concealing or disguising

10. IOIPUSACSU =10. _____
Attended to by favorable circumstances

11. EDOLCDD =11. _____
Treated indulgently; babied

12. ATRULB =12. _____
Cruel or harsh

13. ZDEA =13. _____
Axe-like tool with arched blade at right angles to the handle

14. SLRYAAHD =14. _____
Ropes used to raise or lower a sail or flag

15. DNOOCLNEA =15. _____
Series of columns placed at regular intervals

Odyssey Vocabulary   Juggle Letters 1 Answer Key

1. RELEITPYXP = 1. PERPLEXITY
State of being puzzled or confused

2. RUAGHDENA = 2. HARANGUED
Delivered a long, strong-feeling speech

3. REENPLDDU = 3. PLUNDERED
Robbed of goods by force

4. IOCNALR = 4. CLARION
Shrill and clear

5. TNVEEENBOL = 5. BENEVOLENT
Kind

6. CRFAE = 6. FARCE
Empty show; mockery

7. SERIUDMS = 7. SURMISED
Inferred without conclusive evidence; guessed; gathered

8. TCRIEELD = 8. DERELICT
Vagrant or social outcast

9. OISINTSLIMAUD = 9. DISSIMULATION
Concealing or disguising

10. IOIPUSACSU =10. AUSPICIOUS
Attended to by favorable circumstances

11. EDOLCDD =11. CODDLED
Treated indulgently; babied

12. ATRULB =12. BRUTAL
Cruel or harsh

13. ZDEA =13. ADZE
Axe-like tool with arched blade at right angles to the handle

14. SLRYAAHD =14. HALYARDS
Ropes used to raise or lower a sail or flag

15. DNOOCLNEA =15. COLONNADE
Series of columns placed at regular intervals

Copyrighted

Odyssey Vocabulary   Juggle Letters 2

1. NOLUIUMS = 1. _____
   Emitting self-generated light

2. ETETLF = 2. _____
   Proper or sound condition; good spirits

3. CIAAMELBPL = 3. _____
   Incapable of being pleased

4. URNASAI = 4. _____
   Lizard-like

5. OUIPAUSCIS = 5. _____
   Attended to by favorable circumstances

6. OIATLNCPISUP = 6. _____
   Plea; asking for humbly or earnestly

7. IIANLTGO = 7. _____
   Design incised beneath the surface of metal

8. TFAIDSF = 8. _____
   Stick on a spinning wheel that holds unspun wool

9. CNAGRAROE = 9. _____
   Insolent pride

10. OICLUAMTSA = 10. _____
    Causing or involving a disaster

11. EEAGRM = 11. _____
    Small in quantity, fullness, or extent

12. NOIAIBTL = 12. _____
    Liquid offering as a part of a religious ritual; intoxicating liquid

13. RISSRAOC = 13. _____
    Pirates

14. NTESDIT = 14. _____
    Restricted or limited

15. DESPETE = 15. _____
    Soaked

Odyssey Vocabulary   Juggle Letters 2 Answer Key

1. NOLUIUMS = 1. LUMINOUS
   Emitting self-generated light

2. ETETLF = 2. FETTLE
   Proper or sound condition; good spirits

3. CIAAMELBPL = 3. IMPLACABLE
   Incapable of being pleased

4. URNASAI = 4. SAURIAN
   Lizard-like

5. OUIPAUSCIS = 5. AUSPICIOUS
   Attended to by favorable circumstances

6. OIATLNCPISUP = 6. SUPPLICATION
   Plea; asking for humbly or earnestly

7. IIANLTGO = 7. INTAGLIO
   Design incised beneath the surface of metal

8. TFAIDSF = 8. DISTAFF
   Stick on a spinning wheel that holds unspun wool

9. CNAGRAROE = 9. ARROGANCE
   Insolent pride

10. OICLUAMTSA = 10. CALAMITOUS
    Causing or involving a disaster

11. EEAGRM = 11. MEAGER
    Small in quantity, fullness, or extent

12. NOIAIBTL = 12. LIBATION
    Liquid offering as a part of a religious ritual; intoxicating liquid

13. RISSRAOC = 13. CORSAIRS
    Pirates

14. NTESDIT = 14. STINTED
    Restricted or limited

15. DESPETE = 15. STEEPED
    Soaked

Odyssey Vocabulary  Juggle Letters 3

1. EDNODRIA = 1. _____
Prearranged; predestined

2. FDCREENEE = 2. _____
Courteous respect

3. IUORNPFOS = 3. _____
Abundance; extravagance

4. AASYRLHD = 4. _____
Ropes used to raise or lower a sail or flag

5. BUCDUESMC = 5. _____
Yielded or submitted to an overpowering force

6. ACRONR = 6. _____
Bitter, long-lasting resentment

7. ONRIACL = 7. _____
Shrill and clear

8. EDLTAOSE = 8. _____
Deserted; dreary, gloomy

9. LETPSRE = 9. _____
Sea birds

10. PXIRTEEYPL =10. _____
State of being puzzled or confused

11. LOTFU =11. _____
Show contempt or scorn

12. OSECR =12. _____
Group of twenty items

13. UUYRAG =13. _____
Interpreting signs and omens

14. UYDAACTI =14. _____
Boldness or daring

15. LBIEG =15. _____
Water that collects in the low part of a ship's hull

Odyssey Vocabulary   Juggle Letters 3 Answer Key

1. EDNODRIA = 1. ORDAINED
Prearranged; predestined

2. FDCREENEE = 2. DEFERENCE
Courteous respect

3. IUORNPFOS = 3. PROFUSION
Abundance; extravagance

4. AASYRLHD = 4. HALYARDS
Ropes used to raise or lower a sail or flag

5. BUCDUESMC = 5. SUCCUMBED
Yielded or submitted to an overpowering force

6. ACRONR = 6. RANCOR
Bitter, long-lasting resentment

7. ONRIACL = 7. CLARION
Shrill and clear

8. EDLTAOSE = 8. DESOLATE
Deserted; dreary, gloomy

9. LETPSRE = 9. PETRELS
Sea birds

10. PXIRTEEYPL =10. PERPLEXITY
State of being puzzled or confused

11. LOTFU =11. FLOUT
Show contempt or scorn

12. OSECR =12. SCORE
Group of twenty items

13. UUYRAG =13. AUGURY
Interpreting signs and omens

14. UYDAACTI =14. AUDACITY
Boldness or daring

15. LBIEG =15. BILGE
Water that collects in the low part of a ship's hull

Odyssey Vocabulary  Juggle Letters 4

1. UUOINTSM = 1. _____
   Rebellious

2. UFOLT = 2. _____
   Show contempt or scorn

3. LICVNAGIE = 3. _____
   Watchfulness

4. LSCHETAT = 4. _____
   Articles of personal, movable property; slaves

5. TULRBA = 5. _____
   Cruel or harsh

6. NEADW = 6. _____
   Approached an end

7. OLB = 7. _____
   Hit, toss, or propel in a high arc

8. AIDCYTUA = 8. _____
   Boldness or daring

9. NPROOUSIF = 9. _____
   Abundance; extravagance

10. ASWLARTT =10. _____
    Having physical strength

11. DNOEAYN =11. _____
    Anything that soothes or confronts

12. UVANT =12. _____
    Boast or brag

13. ELPAPDLA =13. _____
    Filled with dismay

14. ECFRA =14. _____
    Empty show; mockery

15. ETNVOLENBE =15. _____
    Kind

Odyssey Vocabulary   Juggle Letters 4

1. UUOINTSM = 1. MUTINOUS
Rebellious

2. UFOLT = 2. FLOUT
Show contempt or scorn

3. LICVNAGIE = 3. VIGILANCE
Watchfulness

4. LSCHETAT = 4. CHATTELS
Articles of personal, movable property; slaves

5. TULRBA = 5. BRUTAL
Cruel or harsh

6. NEADW = 6. WANED
Approached an end

7. OLB = 7. LOB
Hit, toss, or propel in a high arc

8. AIDCYTUA = 8. AUDACITY
Boldness or daring

9. NPROOUSIF = 9. PROFUSION
Abundance; extravagance

10. ASWLARTT =10. STALWART
Having physical strength

11. DNOEAYN =11. ANODYNE
Anything that soothes or confronts

12. UVANT =12. VAUNT
Boast or brag

13. ELPAPDLA =13. APPALLED
Filled with dismay

14. ECFRA =14. FARCE
Empty show; mockery

15. ETNVOLENBE =15. BENEVOLENT
Kind

| | |
|---|---|
| ADZE | Axe-like tool with arched blade at right angles to the handle |
| ANNIHILATION | The act of destroying completely |
| ANODYNE | Anything that soothes or confronts |
| APPALLED | Filled with dismay |
| ARROGANCE | Insolent pride |
| AUDACITY | Boldness or daring |
| AUGURY | Interpreting signs and omens |

| | |
|---|---|
| AUSPICIOUS | Attended to by favorable circumstances |
| BALSAM | Tree that yields an aromatic, sticky substance |
| BENEVOLENT | Kind |
| BIER | Stand on which a coffin or corpse is placed |
| BILGE | Water that collects in the low part of a ship's hull |
| BRACE | A pair |
| BRUTAL | Cruel or harsh |

| | |
|---|---|
| CACHE | Hole or hiding place |
| CALAMITOUS | Causing or involving a disaster |
| CANDOR | Frankness; sincerity |
| CHATTELS | Articles of personal, movable property; slaves |
| CLARION | Shrill and clear |
| CLEFT | Division, separation |
| CODDLED | Treated indulgently; babied |

| | |
|---|---|
| COLLOQUY | Formal conversation |
| COLONNADE | Series of columns placed at regular intervals |
| COMELY | Attractive; handsome; graceful |
| COMPUNCTION | Strong uneasiness caused by a sense of guilt |
| CONTENDING | Striving in battle or controversy |
| CONTENTIOUSLY | In a quarrelsome way |
| CORSAIRS | Pirates |

| | |
|---|---|
| CRANING | Stretching and straining |
| DEFERENCE | Courteous respect |
| DERELICT | Vagrant or social outcast |
| DESOLATE | Deserted; dreary, gloomy |
| DISPERSED | Scattered in different directions |
| DISSIMULATION | Concealing or disguising |
| DISTAFF | Stick on a spinning wheel that holds unspun wool |

| | |
|---|---|
| DOLE | Distribute in small portions |
| FARCE | Empty show; mockery |
| FEIGN | Pretend |
| FETTLE | Proper or sound condition; good spirits |
| FLOUT | Show contempt or scorn |
| GUILE | Craftiness |
| HALYARDS | Ropes used to raise or lower a sail or flag |

| | |
|---|---|
| HAPLESS | Luckless; unfortunate |
| HARANGUED | Delivered a long, strong-feeling speech |
| HOVERED | Floated as if suspended |
| IMPLACABLE | Incapable of being pleased |
| INTAGLIO | Design incised beneath the surface of metal |
| LIBATION | Liquid offering as a part of a religious ritual; intoxicating liquid |
| LOB | Hit, toss, or propel in a high arc |

| | |
|---|---|
| LUMINOUS | Emitting self-generated light |
| MEAGER | Small in quantity, fullness, or extent |
| MINIONS | Employees or domestic servants |
| MORTIFIED | Shamed or humiliated |
| MUSTER | Assemble or gather together |
| MUTINOUS | Rebellious |
| OBLIVION | State of being completely forgotten |

| | |
|---|---|
| OBSTINACY | Stubbornness |
| ORDAINED | Prearranged; predestined |
| PATRIMONY | Inheritance from a father |
| PERPLEXITY | State of being puzzled or confused |
| PETRELS | Sea birds |
| PITH | Essential or central part of anything |
| PLUNDERED | Robbed of goods by force |

| | |
|---|---|
| PRECEDENCE | Priority; going in advance |
| PREVAILS | Triumphs or wins |
| PRODIGIOUS | Impressively great in size |
| PROFUSION | Abundance; extravagance |
| PROMONTORY | High ridge of land or rock jutting into the sea |
| PROWESS | Superior skill or ability |
| PUNGENT | A sharp, bitter taste |

| | |
|---|---|
| RANCOR | Bitter, long-lasting resentment |
| REBUKE | Criticize sharply |
| RESPLENDENT | Brilliant |
| RETAINER | Subordinates of an organization or an individual |
| SAURIAN | Lizard-like |
| SCORE | Group of twenty items |
| STALWART | Having physical strength |

| | |
|---|---|
| STEEPED | Soaked |
| STINTED | Restricted or limited |
| SUCCUMBED | Yielded or submitted to an overpowering force |
| SUPPLICATION | Plea; asking for humbly or earnestly |
| SURMISED | Inferred without conclusive evidence; guessed; gathered |
| TACTICIAN | A person skilled in maneuvering |
| TAUT | Pulled or drawn tight |

| | |
|---|---|
| TIMOROUS | Apprehensive; fearfully cautious |
| TUMULT | Disorderly commotion |
| TYRO | Beginner or inexperienced person |
| VALOR | Courage and boldness |
| VAUNT | Boast or brag |
| VIE | To compete or strive for victory |
| VIGILANCE | Watchfulness |

| | |
|---|---|
| VIVACITY | Liveliness |
| WANED | Approached an end |
| WIELDING | Handling a weapon or a tool |
| WINDFALL | Sudden and unexpected piece of good fortune |

## Odyssey Vocabulary

| | | | | |
|---|---|---|---|---|
| ADZE | AUDACITY | GUILE | CHATTELS | BRUTAL |
| PRECEDENCE | CODDLED | LUMINOUS | SCORE | PATRIMONY |
| SUPPLICATION | TIMOROUS | FREE SPACE | SUCCUMBED | CLARION |
| BILGE | DERELICT | MEAGER | TUMULT | MUSTER |
| PROMONTORY | HOVERED | OBSTINACY | PETRELS | FETTLE |

## Odyssey Vocabulary

| | | | | |
|---|---|---|---|---|
| LOB | OBLIVION | CONTENDING | CACHE | VIE |
| STEEPED | VAUNT | VIVACITY | SURMISED | ARROGANCE |
| FARCE | FLOUT | FREE SPACE | CALAMITOUS | DESOLATE |
| CORSAIRS | COLLOQUY | FEIGN | PLUNDERED | DOLE |
| AUGURY | LIBATION | MINIONS | BENEVOLENT | VIGILANCE |

Odyssey Vocabulary

| MEAGER | MINIONS | COMELY | VIVACITY | COLLOQUY |
|---|---|---|---|---|
| CLEFT | CRANING | SAURIAN | TACTICIAN | FARCE |
| PERPLEXITY | CACHE | FREE SPACE | WIELDING | CODDLED |
| PUNGENT | ORDAINED | PROWESS | PLUNDERED | WINDFALL |
| VIE | IMPLACABLE | ADZE | PRECEDENCE | BIER |

Odyssey Vocabulary

| COLONNADE | TYRO | BRUTAL | CONTENDING | PETRELS |
|---|---|---|---|---|
| RANCOR | DERELICT | TUMULT | SURMISED | HAPLESS |
| VAUNT | FLOUT | FREE SPACE | DISSIMULATION | AUSPICIOUS |
| BENEVOLENT | ANNIHILATION | HALYARDS | PATRIMONY | AUGURY |
| TIMOROUS | TAUT | FETTLE | VALOR | BALSAM |

## Odyssey Vocabulary

| | | | | |
|---|---|---|---|---|
| BIER | SAURIAN | COMPUNCTION | RESPLENDENT | PROMONTORY |
| PREVAILS | FLOUT | DOLE | RETAINER | BRACE |
| DISTAFF | COLLOQUY | FREE SPACE | REBUKE | PUNGENT |
| VIVACITY | SUCCUMBED | TIMOROUS | HARANGUED | CALAMITOUS |
| VIE | TACTICIAN | BILGE | CACHE | PRODIGIOUS |

## Odyssey Vocabulary

| | | | | |
|---|---|---|---|---|
| MEAGER | BRUTAL | CLEFT | CONTENDING | AUDACITY |
| APPALLED | MORTIFIED | ORDAINED | RANCOR | FARCE |
| COLONNADE | PATRIMONY | FREE SPACE | WANED | INTAGLIO |
| DESOLATE | SCORE | DISPERSED | DERELICT | CRANING |
| PROWESS | PROFUSION | ARROGANCE | ANODYNE | PETRELS |

## Odyssey Vocabulary

| PRECEDENCE | TYRO | LIBATION | RETAINER | HOVERED |
|---|---|---|---|---|
| RESPLENDENT | WINDFALL | OBSTINACY | WIELDING | PROMONTORY |
| PETRELS | PLUNDERED | FREE SPACE | DERELICT | CONTENTIOUSLY |
| CORSAIRS | DISSIMULATION | AUDACITY | BRACE | FLOUT |
| DISTAFF | PROWESS | CHATTELS | COMPUNCTION | INTAGLIO |

## Odyssey Vocabulary

| SUPPLICATION | SCORE | PROFUSION | SAURIAN | RANCOR |
|---|---|---|---|---|
| REBUKE | CALAMITOUS | STALWART | HARANGUED | VIE |
| ADZE | CACHE | FREE SPACE | BRUTAL | ANNIHILATION |
| AUSPICIOUS | ANODYNE | CANDOR | DESOLATE | TUMULT |
| DEFERENCE | VIVACITY | OBLIVION | ARROGANCE | STINTED |

## Odyssey Vocabulary

| DEFERENCE | SUPPLICATION | SURMISED | PETRELS | LUMINOUS |
|---|---|---|---|---|
| FARCE | RANCOR | CALAMITOUS | DISSIMULATION | TAUT |
| OBLIVION | ARROGANCE | FREE SPACE | STALWART | PERPLEXITY |
| MORTIFIED | RETAINER | MINIONS | BILGE | APPALLED |
| VIGILANCE | AUSPICIOUS | COMPUNCTION | PATRIMONY | MUTINOUS |

## Odyssey Vocabulary

| COLONNADE | LIBATION | OBSTINACY | BRACE | MUSTER |
|---|---|---|---|---|
| CONTENTIOUSLY | VIE | PRECEDENCE | WINDFALL | TIMOROUS |
| ORDAINED | BRUTAL | FREE SPACE | HARANGUED | HAPLESS |
| GUILE | WANED | PLUNDERED | COLLOQUY | DESOLATE |
| CODDLED | VAUNT | AUGURY | PUNGENT | TACTICIAN |

## Odyssey Vocabulary

| MORTIFIED | FEIGN | TYRO | APPALLED | VIE |
|---|---|---|---|---|
| CALAMITOUS | INTAGLIO | HOVERED | BALSAM | AUSPICIOUS |
| PETRELS | OBSTINACY | FREE SPACE | MUTINOUS | CLARION |
| AUDACITY | PERPLEXITY | COMELY | PATRIMONY | DISPERSED |
| BRUTAL | FETTLE | VIGILANCE | STEEPED | BILGE |

## Odyssey Vocabulary

| CHATTELS | CACHE | WINDFALL | CONTENTIOUSLY | PROFUSION |
|---|---|---|---|---|
| SAURIAN | IMPLACABLE | ORDAINED | OBLIVION | ANNIHILATION |
| STINTED | PREVAILS | FREE SPACE | COLONNADE | RETAINER |
| WANED | FARCE | CRANING | DISTAFF | LUMINOUS |
| SCORE | BENEVOLENT | WIELDING | TAUT | SURMISED |

## Odyssey Vocabulary

| | | | | |
|---|---|---|---|---|
| SURMISED | STALWART | LIBATION | OBSTINACY | WINDFALL |
| PATRIMONY | VALOR | PITH | ANODYNE | CRANING |
| DISSIMULATION | CORSAIRS | FREE SPACE | DEFERENCE | IMPLACABLE |
| PROWESS | CLARION | COLLOQUY | OBLIVION | TAUT |
| DERELICT | VIGILANCE | WANED | FEIGN | DISTAFF |

## Odyssey Vocabulary

| | | | | |
|---|---|---|---|---|
| CODDLED | LOB | RESPLENDENT | HOVERED | DESOLATE |
| ANNIHILATION | FLOUT | MEAGER | RANCOR | BRUTAL |
| MORTIFIED | COMPUNCTION | FREE SPACE | VIVACITY | AUDACITY |
| TACTICIAN | COLONNADE | TYRO | APPALLED | PERPLEXITY |
| LUMINOUS | HAPLESS | PETRELS | WIELDING | MUTINOUS |

## Odyssey Vocabulary

| VIE | HARANGUED | VIGILANCE | BILGE | CONTENDING |
|---|---|---|---|---|
| MUSTER | OBSTINACY | CLEFT | DISPERSED | PREVAILS |
| BRUTAL | DERELICT | FREE SPACE | VALOR | RANCOR |
| SUPPLICATION | INTAGLIO | MINIONS | CODDLED | CRANING |
| MORTIFIED | TAUT | WIELDING | FARCE | MEAGER |

## Odyssey Vocabulary

| CANDOR | PUNGENT | COLONNADE | FETTLE | DISTAFF |
|---|---|---|---|---|
| VIVACITY | CHATTELS | OBLIVION | FEIGN | LOB |
| CONTENTIOUSLY | BALSAM | FREE SPACE | PROWESS | COLLOQUY |
| LIBATION | SCORE | PROMONTORY | GUILE | CLARION |
| STALWART | COMPUNCTION | ARROGANCE | HAPLESS | STINTED |

**Odyssey Vocabulary**

| RETAINER | VIGILANCE | PRODIGIOUS | CONTENTIOUSLY | APPALLED |
|---|---|---|---|---|
| MORTIFIED | CODDLED | FEIGN | CACHE | TACTICIAN |
| PATRIMONY | PROMONTORY | FREE SPACE | AUGURY | TUMULT |
| COMELY | CORSAIRS | FLOUT | LUMINOUS | PRECEDENCE |
| PITH | MUTINOUS | COMPUNCTION | IMPLACABLE | BENEVOLENT |

**Odyssey Vocabulary**

| AUSPICIOUS | CALAMITOUS | STALWART | BILGE | OBSTINACY |
|---|---|---|---|---|
| STEEPED | BIER | CHATTELS | HAPLESS | VAUNT |
| SAURIAN | TYRO | FREE SPACE | PREVAILS | CLEFT |
| DEFERENCE | CONTENDING | MEAGER | VALOR | TAUT |
| RESPLENDENT | PERPLEXITY | WINDFALL | SUPPLICATION | MUSTER |

## Odyssey Vocabulary

| COMPUNCTION | WIELDING | PREVAILS | BALSAM | TACTICIAN |
|---|---|---|---|---|
| COLONNADE | CONTENTIOUSLY | DOLE | MEAGER | CRANING |
| OBSTINACY | CLEFT | FREE SPACE | VALOR | TAUT |
| FETTLE | CALAMITOUS | CONTENDING | CLARION | ANODYNE |
| AUDACITY | SUCCUMBED | PRODIGIOUS | CORSAIRS | INTAGLIO |

## Odyssey Vocabulary

| AUGURY | DISSIMULATION | OBLIVION | AUSPICIOUS | PERPLEXITY |
|---|---|---|---|---|
| FARCE | ARROGANCE | BIER | VIVACITY | PATRIMONY |
| BENEVOLENT | PROFUSION | FREE SPACE | ANNIHILATION | VIE |
| IMPLACABLE | RESPLENDENT | PUNGENT | VIGILANCE | GUILE |
| COLLOQUY | HALYARDS | DISPERSED | PROWESS | SUPPLICATION |

## Odyssey Vocabulary

| | | | | |
|---|---|---|---|---|
| ANODYNE | GUILE | SCORE | CACHE | DEFERENCE |
| CLARION | CONTENTIOUSLY | COMELY | MUTINOUS | INTAGLIO |
| RETAINER | ORDAINED | FREE SPACE | TAUT | STEEPED |
| CRANING | SUPPLICATION | PITH | PATRIMONY | CORSAIRS |
| TIMOROUS | AUSPICIOUS | APPALLED | MINIONS | HALYARDS |

## Odyssey Vocabulary

| | | | | |
|---|---|---|---|---|
| DOLE | DISPERSED | BILGE | SURMISED | WINDFALL |
| STINTED | SUCCUMBED | FETTLE | BIER | PERPLEXITY |
| AUGURY | TYRO | FREE SPACE | TACTICIAN | ADZE |
| COLONNADE | SAURIAN | DISTAFF | COLLOQUY | FARCE |
| MUSTER | DERELICT | MORTIFIED | IMPLACABLE | DISSIMULATION |

## Odyssey Vocabulary

| BRACE | CORSAIRS | OBLIVION | RANCOR | LUMINOUS |
|---|---|---|---|---|
| WIELDING | PROMONTORY | INTAGLIO | SUCCUMBED | MUTINOUS |
| CONTENDING | REBUKE | FREE SPACE | AUSPICIOUS | DEFERENCE |
| COLLOQUY | PITH | HALYARDS | BALSAM | DISSIMULATION |
| ARROGANCE | MEAGER | TACTICIAN | SCORE | CODDLED |

## Odyssey Vocabulary

| PROWESS | IMPLACABLE | MINIONS | PRECEDENCE | BILGE |
|---|---|---|---|---|
| CACHE | AUGURY | BIER | VAUNT | DISTAFF |
| BRUTAL | VIE | FREE SPACE | LIBATION | PROFUSION |
| HARANGUED | ADZE | WINDFALL | STEEPED | SUPPLICATION |
| GUILE | STINTED | RESPLENDENT | MORTIFIED | PLUNDERED |

## Odyssey Vocabulary

| MUTINOUS | FARCE | TIMOROUS | FEIGN | DEFERENCE |
|---|---|---|---|---|
| DOLE | MEAGER | WIELDING | BIER | VIVACITY |
| RANCOR | BILGE | FREE SPACE | PITH | COLLOQUY |
| CANDOR | DERELICT | MORTIFIED | SURMISED | DISSIMULATION |
| DESOLATE | INTAGLIO | ANODYNE | STINTED | CLARION |

## Odyssey Vocabulary

| CRANING | CHATTELS | ADZE | HOVERED | CODDLED |
|---|---|---|---|---|
| SUCCUMBED | HAPLESS | PROMONTORY | CORSAIRS | LIBATION |
| APPALLED | LOB | FREE SPACE | COMELY | TYRO |
| SUPPLICATION | WANED | BALSAM | CALAMITOUS | PETRELS |
| FLOUT | CACHE | COMPUNCTION | STALWART | HALYARDS |

## Odyssey Vocabulary

| | | | | |
|---|---|---|---|---|
| CODDLED | SCORE | MUSTER | COLLOQUY | TIMOROUS |
| BENEVOLENT | CANDOR | CLARION | TAUT | TYRO |
| AUSPICIOUS | RANCOR | FREE SPACE | PITH | STALWART |
| INTAGLIO | PROMONTORY | CORSAIRS | WINDFALL | PREVAILS |
| CACHE | VAUNT | VIE | HAPLESS | WANED |

## Odyssey Vocabulary

| | | | | |
|---|---|---|---|---|
| PRECEDENCE | DISTAFF | ANODYNE | HARANGUED | FETTLE |
| WIELDING | CRANING | PRODIGIOUS | DISSIMULATION | OBLIVION |
| REBUKE | AUDACITY | FREE SPACE | FARCE | ARROGANCE |
| FLOUT | DOLE | DESOLATE | HALYARDS | PERPLEXITY |
| DERELICT | IMPLACABLE | RETAINER | VIVACITY | DEFERENCE |

## Odyssey Vocabulary

| | | | | |
|---|---|---|---|---|
| SAURIAN | IMPLACABLE | BRUTAL | SUPPLICATION | REBUKE |
| MUSTER | VIVACITY | FLOUT | ARROGANCE | FEIGN |
| DERELICT | VIE | FREE SPACE | RESPLENDENT | ORDAINED |
| LUMINOUS | CLARION | LIBATION | BIER | OBLIVION |
| PATRIMONY | GUILE | DISSIMULATION | CALAMITOUS | MORTIFIED |

## Odyssey Vocabulary

| | | | | |
|---|---|---|---|---|
| AUDACITY | DISTAFF | COMPUNCTION | COLONNADE | HALYARDS |
| CANDOR | MUTINOUS | PETRELS | HARANGUED | WIELDING |
| TUMULT | MEAGER | FREE SPACE | PROFUSION | DESOLATE |
| TAUT | PRECEDENCE | BILGE | COLLOQUY | SURMISED |
| PUNGENT | MINIONS | VIGILANCE | WINDFALL | PITH |

## Odyssey Vocabulary

| LUMINOUS | ANNIHILATION | CACHE | PRECEDENCE | VAUNT |
|---|---|---|---|---|
| MORTIFIED | MEAGER | ORDAINED | HALYARDS | HAPLESS |
| SUPPLICATION | FEIGN | FREE SPACE | MUSTER | ARROGANCE |
| VIVACITY | SURMISED | PROFUSION | WIELDING | WINDFALL |
| VIE | HARANGUED | TACTICIAN | CONTENDING | RESPLENDENT |

## Odyssey Vocabulary

| FARCE | PROMONTORY | MINIONS | DISPERSED | ADZE |
|---|---|---|---|---|
| INTAGLIO | AUGURY | LOB | BALSAM | TUMULT |
| CODDLED | AUDACITY | FREE SPACE | PLUNDERED | COLLOQUY |
| STALWART | CONTENTIOUSLY | OBLIVION | CALAMITOUS | PETRELS |
| IMPLACABLE | SUCCUMBED | STEEPED | SAURIAN | DESOLATE |

www.ingramcontent.com/pod-product-compliance
Lightning Source LLC
Chambersburg PA
CBHW081453070526
44586CB00019B/2331